LETTING OFF STEAM

Letting Off Steam

LETTING OFF STEAM

Letting Off Steam

A brief history of a Royal Navy Artificer
turned boiler installer in South Africa

Jeffrey Deacon

LETTING OFF STEAM

LETTING OFF STEAM

Copyright © Jeffrey Deacon 2023

All rights reserved

ISBN: 979-8-8720-3570-1

LETTING OFF STEAM

Table of contents

Early days	9
Schooling	17
The Royal Navy	24
The Real Navy & Sea-going Ships	33
Return to the UK	46
The joy of the Garden route	53
Emigration	73
The Construction Industry	81
East London	104
A change of direction	113
Second visit to the UK	127
Self-Employment	134
Permanent return to the UK	147
Scotland	154
A range of jobs	161
Tragedy	172
How much longer?	179

LETTING OFF STEAM

Chapter 1

Early days

Youngster

It was Saturday 16th May 1936, and I was born with a hare lip in the small village of Ryeford near Ross-on-Wye in Herefordshire, in the house across the road from my grandparent's home, the Barker house, Rose Cottage. The doctor carried out an operation to correct the hare lip within days and made the comment that, "he can always grow a moustache to hide it". It was something that made me very self-conscious and shy for years.

I don't know how long it was before I became a resident of my grandparent's house because being the son of a sailor in the Royal Navy, we moved around quite a lot. My father, Harry Jeffrey Deacon, was a submariner and as Britain's submarine base was HMS Dolphin in Gosport, it wasn't long before we were living in that town.

I have no idea of my age at this particular time, but my earliest real recollection of life was while we were living in Dunoon in Scotland where my Dad's submarine was based alongside a depot ship there. There may be other incidents that come to mind before this time, but I do not have dates other than my Dad's service record to verify the chronological order of everything.

I understand that I was four and a half years old when I started school for the first time and that was while we lived in Dunoon in Scotland. I had to find my own way there as my mother was in service as a cook and my dad was at sea so there was nobody to take me.

After school each day I had to go to the premises where my mother was a cook. One day the belt from my raincoat was found in the grounds but no sign of me! It must have caused quite a stir as the Police were called and a search of Dunoon was started, including the Fire Service, for one little boy. It went on for the rest of the day and after dark when the said little boy was found wedged behind a pillar-box on the loch side, completely engrossed, watching a group of sailors with a boat in the water and totally unaware of everyone's concern!

Last days with my father

The depot ship, HMS Forth I think, and her submarines were an obvious target for the Luftwaffe, and I remember "taking cover" in the house we shared and rented with another RN family during bombing raids. I don't recall any successful hits for the bombers. There were times too where I ran along the road and down the pier to meet Dad when he came ashore with other liberty men. This was after spotting the submarine HMS/M Talisman with the pennant number N78, sailing up the loch to the depot ship after a patrol. Our house was right on the edge of the loch so anything that moved in the loch was in plain view for us. These were the last times I was to ever see my father as he was killed aboard his next boat HMS/M Perseus, in the Ionian Sea where she struck a mine one night while charging batteries and sank. It was 6th December 1941. There was one survivor, and this event is well documented on the Internet.

I had my second birthday in Malta where my dad had a married accompanied draft and during this time, I'm told I met Admiral Sir Andrew Cunningham, Commander in Chief (C-in-C) of the Mediterranean Fleet. He came to my second birthday party. I do not remember anything of the time we spent in Malta although my mother loved it. I have been told that on another occasion, I put the fear of God into my family by walking along the top of the balustrading around the top of the house (not the place for a two-year-old) where we lived! One wrong step would have changed my life forever, even terminated it.

"Where's Jeff?" she said and Grampy, looking in the rear-view mirror said, "There he is, lying in the road"!

Another time that has been related to me where I have the vaguest of memory as I do not know my age at the time. I was being driven to Ross in Grampy's car, along with Thelma and Aunt Gwen, to have my hair cut. Gwen, who was sitting in the front passenger seat, turned round to see Thelma and me only to find I wasn't there! "Where's Jeff?" she said and Grampy, looking in the rear-view mirror said, "There he is, lying in the road"!

It is assumed that I accidentally leaned on the door handle, opened the door, and fell out of the car! Knowing now how my grandfather drove and the whereabouts of the car at the time, the vehicle would have been travelling at 30 mph and I ended up in hospital instead of the barber shop where six stitches were put in the back of my head.

Ryeford

I remember my mother receiving the news that my father was reported missing with the loss of HMS/M Perseus while we were living in my grandparent's house. I can only recall living there up to the age of eleven at which time I was shipped off to a boarding school although I understand my mother and me did live in other properties in the area occasionally, and home became a flat at Knights Hill, The Lea, eventually.

My cousin Thelma also lived in my grandparents' home, and we were raised together much like brother and sister mainly by our grandparents as our mothers were at work. Each morning after breakfast both of us would ride our bicycles, independently on different routes, to deliver daily newspapers around the area, before we went to school in Weston-under-Penyard approximately one mile away.

On Thelma's first day at school, I had to take her there, as her big brother, at the age of six! The school had two playgrounds, one for boys and the other for girls and when playtime came, Thelma refused point blank to stay on her own on the girl's side or mix with the other girls, so she was allowed to sit with me in the boy's playground, which meant I couldn't join in the games being played. This was only allowed on her first day and I don't recall any future problems in that direction.

On weekends and holiday time one of us would deliver the newspapers on foot to local residents who lived nearby in the village after we had done our normal tour on the bicycle. This included walking up to the farm with their newspapers and bringing back our milk in a small open can which we would swing round and round vertically on the way back, without the milk spilling out. At least, I never knew it to spill out and I dread to think what would have happened at home if it had done. There was no urgency for these activities and I'm sure some people wondered at what time they would receive the newspapers on Saturdays. We were not required to deliver on Sundays.

There was a different routine on a Sunday. Thinking back now, I do not know why I didn't ride my bike to church as it was the church of St Lawrence in Weston-under-Penyard where I used to sing in the choir. That would be for the morning service around 11:00 and quite often I was the only one in the family that was there for that. It would be home for lunch and then walk back to the church for Sunday school, where Thelma's mother used to teach, and again later for the evening service at 06:30.

My grandfather, affectionately known as Grampy, used to own the village shop although there was no display window. He used to sell cigarettes and tobacco, confectionery, and soft drinks. He also ran a haulage business with his two flatbed lorries. I had to pass through the passageway from the front door where the stock was kept/displayed, to get to the stairs and up to my bedroom.

There was a great temptation to help myself to sweets that were kept in that area, on my way to bed! I'm sure the adults knew this, but I only remember being "caught" once when Thelma and I were outside, and I gave a sweet to Thelma just as we were called in for Tea. It was quite obvious that Thelma was eating something, and she was asked what it was and where had she got it, with the reply," From Jeff"!!! This was during the Second World War when sugar, sweets, etc. plus a lot of other things, were on ration. Normally each of us received a quarter (4oz) of sweets per week as our ration.

There were eight of us living in the Barker house. Grampy and Granny, my mother Emily and me, aunt Doris and Thelma, aunt Gwen and uncle Bert and later Granny's brother uncle John joined us. I don't know how the accommodation was managed as the occasional visitor was always welcome and could stay.

At one time my cousin Ron Deacon, was evacuated from London during the War to the house and attended Weston school with us. His grandmother was accommodated when she came to visit him. I remember that occasion well as American convoys of soldiers used to pass through the village and throw out packets of chewing gum and sweets to the children standing at the roadside. Ron's grandmother made me hand over everything I had managed to catch to Ron, and I was not best pleased about it.

Another of my mother's sisters, Gladys, was in service as a housemaid to an elderly lady who lived in a property about half a mile away from the village called Elm Cottage. Both Thelma and I were invited to tea occasionally with Aunt Glad and we had to have an audience with the elderly lady while we were there. I used to find it quite an unnerving experience as she was always dressed in black and had a glass eye and you were never sure if she was looking at you or not.

Christmas at Ryeford

I'm sure that at some time Grampy's home had been two semi-detached houses because there were two staircases, one at each end of the house. This became very useful at Christmas time when the extended family used to gather in the family home and a large number of people were present. One of the men would suggest a visit to the local public house and all of them would leave all the ladies and children in the "Front room".

The men would accumulate in the kitchen where one of them would dress up as Father Christmas and climb the nearest stairs, stamp through all the bedrooms and descend the second staircase into the Front room. All the Christmas presents that had accumulated under the Christmas tree were then distributed by Father Christmas.

I still do not understand how so many people could fit into that Front room to create the magic of Christmas for us children. I have never experienced any other Christmases like it, they were just Magic.

It was so very different from Christmas of today when on Christmas Eve, Thelma and I got the job of decorating the Christmas tree. During the year our parents deposited money in a Christmas club for us and maybe two weeks before the Day, each of us was given the cash and we were required to go shopping to buy a gift for every family member, so everyone got a gift from us personally. I remember some of the gifts were not very exciting! We also had the job of undressing the tree after the twelve days of Christmas had passed and putting away the decorations until next year.

If there was a village fete the Barkers were usually involved in it in some way and Thelma and I were required to dress up in fancy dress. Both of us detested it but usually we would win a place of some sort. I don't know if there is any association with it, but I used to loathe the annual pantomime visit.

Boarding School

The age of eleven was the time to change from junior to senior school and we were required to sit an examination called the Eleven Plus. This would determine whether we were to attend a Grammar school or some other kind of Secondary school. I became the first person from the Barker house to pass the Eleven Plus after quite a lot of coaching at home with the homework even though I did not think I would make it.

I was one of three pupils that passed from Weston-under-Penyard Junior School, but I did not attend the Grammar school in Ross-on-Wye. I do not know why I was earmarked to go to a boarding school although I suspect that my mother's employment in an ammunition factory in Hereford must have had a bearing and with me away it would ease the load on my grandparents.

I was always led to believe that my father's wish was that I would join the Royal Navy, but with a peaked cap. The choices then were as a naval officer, an Artificer, a writer, a cook or a sick berth attendant and I am sure he would have preferred me to be one of the first two.

Chapter 2

Schooling

The Royal Hospital School

The Royal Hospital School (RHS) is a boarding school in Suffolk for boys and was originally for sons of seafarers from the Royal Navy. The school uniform was based on the number one uniform of a seaman in the Royal Navy and worn on Divisions on Sunday parades. A working uniform of a white RN seaman's shirt, navy short blue trousers and a navy-blue sweater were worn on a daily basis.

So, the day came that I had to go to The Royal Hospital School near Ipswich in Suffolk, and I was escorted on the train by my uncle Bert to London Liverpool Street station to catch the special train to Ipswich.

It appeared to me that my family and friends were on the other side of the country, and I was not at all happy about this and over the next few days I suffered from homesickness. In fact, I was so upset about it that I did the best I could to give the wrong answers to the questions (thinking that I knew the correct answer!) on the entrance exam paper, fail it and get sent back home. I didn't do a very good job because the school ran four streams titled A to D with forms numbered 1 to 6 and I ended up in class1B! The A stream was deemed to be the one with the more intelligent boys.

In my early years Nelson house was not occupied and differed from the others structurally in that it had a dome on it, topped with a weathervane, and stood at the East end of the school facing the avenue between the other ten houses.

These were divided into two blocks of five with three on the top level and two on the lower one and separated by the parade ground. Each house was two stories high in the shape of the letter H with the senior boys living on one side and the juniors on the other with the ablutions and housemasters' accommodation in the centre.

All the houses were named after famous English seafarers and I was made a resident of Blake house; one of five houses on the West side of the school on the lower level, containing approximately sixty boys aged 11 to 16, which would be my home for the next five years, with Mr Eric Pringle as the housemaster who was also a science teacher.

There was also a nursing sister resident in the house who acted as a housekeeper and cared for our minor medical needs and anything more serious was dealt with in the school infirmary. I spent about three weeks in the infirmary one Easter term, in isolation with Chickenpox!

Awards at school

After becoming the top student of 1B at the end of the first year, on Speech Day I was pleased to collect my prize, along with the other prize winners, from the headmaster, on stage in front of the assembled school plus my mother and other guests.

I was promoted into class 2A for the following year. This caused a couple of problems for me as the 'B' stream did not teach French or Seamanship and I did not do well at either of these new subjects at all and was behind the others who had started in 1A. Our French teacher was Mr

Cross, who also taught us History and because of my dislike of French, History wasn't a favourite either!

... and I found the signals instructor somewhat overpowering particularly with Morse code.

The following year in 3A, French was taught by Mr Foster who had an entirely different approach of presenting the subject and I excelled at it. I never recovered an interest in History until I became an adult in later life. I was to stay in the 'A' stream for the rest of my time at the school.

The school taught Seamanship, a subject unknown in most schools, and my first lesson did not enamour me to it at all. The instructors were all ex Royal Navy retired Chief Petty Officers and I found the signals instructor somewhat overpowering particularly with Morse code.

I did not look forward to Seamanship classes after that but as time went by, I decided that it was not going to go away and I asked my mother for a seamanship manual, which I still have, and put extra effort into learning as much as I could about it and as the years passed, I became quite proficient.

In my final year I took the test for a signals badge and achieved 98% for Morse code, 100% for Signal Flags and sadly, 12% for Semaphore! The problem with that was that you needed an assistant while reading Semaphore, someone else had to write it down and in those days, there wasn't, or we were not taught, the phonetic alphabet. While I spoke the letters and numerals that I read, something entirely different was being written down (perhaps my diction was not so good!). In the end we were allowed a few minutes to make any adjustments necessary and I managed to decipher enough of the message to earn the 12%!

There was also the Suffolk prize for the top student in Seamanship in the school and I had become the favourite to win it. However, the test was held while I was away at Lee-on-Solent taking part in an aptitude test for an apprenticeship prior to joining the Royal Navy, which was disappointing.

To the east side of the school there was a boathouse at the creek that led on to the river Stour where the school had several boats. To reach the river a knowledge of the channel in the creek was necessary and to gain this special knowledge a test was required. Having passed the test, you were recognised as a coxswain and a lanyard could be worn with the school uniform.

I was proud to wear my lanyard, and the crossed rifles badge on my left sleeve cuff as a marksman, being captain of the school shooting team for a couple of years. There were boat races between the various houses, but these were not the light boats we see on Boat Race Day on the Thames. Our boats were full size RN whalers!

In my final year I was promoted to Petty Officer boy. This was in the position of Prefect, and I took up my position on the Junior side of Blake house with another Petty Officer boy. We were responsible for keeping order on that side of the building and marching the juniors wherever they had to go, i.e., the dining hall for meals, the parade ground for Divisions and the chapel each morning before classes.

Generally, you did not just walk anywhere, and everything was regulated much the same as the Royal Navy! Divisions were held every Sunday on the parade ground, we would be required to be dressed in our full school uniform, each house assembled in three columns and an inspection carried out as in the RN and marched off to the chapel to the music of the school brass band.

After morning service, we would reassemble on the lower road on the east side to march past the central dais on the parade ground where Major Buckley (ex-Royal Marines) would take the salute with the headmaster.

Every morning we were woken at 06:45 to go into the communal showers and after making our beds we would be assigned individual duties of housework. Generally, these were tasks such as polishing the brightwork in the toilets, cleaning the shower rooms, sweeping the stairs and landing, also the cloisters and the outside assembly area and the dormitory and dayroom.

Once a week we would polish the floor in the dormitory after cleaners had laid wax polish for us to produce a shine. We stripped our beds on Saturday mornings and remade them in the afternoon with clean linen, hospital corners of course!

After we had performed our daily duties, we would fall in in the assembly area and march to the dining hall for breakfast and having eaten, we could walk back to our houses independently. Then, once again we would fall in and march to the chapel for morning service before going to our various classrooms. Another march to the dining hall for lunch followed by afternoon lessons in the classrooms and the routine for the evening meal was virtually the same again.

Wednesdays were slightly different as we would take part in games on the playing fields in the afternoon. Only inclement weather interfered with this routine, when we were allowed to stay in the day room, otherwise everyone played games, and nobody was excused. If you didn't play, you watched! Twice per week we would have prep classes for two hours after the evening meal.

There were occasions when a boy would run away from school and the police would be required to bring him back! Although I did not like the existence we had at school, I never considered running away, and it would have been around one hundred miles to home anyway which would have been daunting.

Weekends

Saturday and Sunday differed slightly with lessons during the forenoon on Saturday the same as other days but once again we played sport in the afternoon unless the weather was against us. In the evenings we were treated to a film or a lecture in the Assembly Hall. No one was excused unless they were on punishment such as detention.

On Sundays we took part in Divisions and church services morning and evening. I was confirmed when I was thirteen by the bishop of Bury St Edmunds and became an altar server soon afterwards. It was the only day that we were allowed out of the school premises for a limited amount of time wearing the school uniform and even this was restricted as to how many of us could go out at a time. There was little choice once outside, usually Mr Gobbet's shop at the bottom of the hill, unless a relative came to visit when we could be escorted further afield.

Sport

I have always been keen to play football and Blake House was a little above average when it came to inter-house competition. Although I ended up a long way from home, I was rather pleased that I did not go to the Grammar School in Ross-on-Wye as rugby was played there in preference to football. I knew nothing about rugby except that it appeared to be a rough and aggressive game and I did not wish to take part.

At RHS we played football during the Christmas term, rugby in the Easter term and cricket and athletics during the Summer term. I am still no cricket fan, but I used to be a useful sprinter and enjoyed attaining the standard or better in all the athletic disciplines every year.

I had to play rugby and once the rules and method were explained to me, I really enjoyed the game. In fact, in my final year Blake House were unbeatable and we won every game we played with me playing as a wing three-quarter.

Also, in the Easter term we took part in cross country running, not a favourite of mine as I preferred the faster, shorter events. Even so, I did not do too badly at it and usually finished in the top fifteen in the inter-house events. The school had its own gymnasium and swimming bath and all of us were taught to swim with inter-house competition during the Summer term.

Chapter 3
The Royal Navy

Joining up

The school was a regular supplier of candidates for the Royal Naval Artificer apprenticeship examination, and I joined a number of boys to sit the examination when today's children are sitting their General Certificate of Education.

I passed the examination along with a few other boys and had to spend several days at the naval base at HMS Daedalus at Lee-on-the-Solent, doing an aptitude test. Some of the resulting efforts were quite amusing and obviously meant failure for the individual who supplied it! I was very pleased to find that I was accepted, and I could study to become what my Dad had hoped would be the career I would follow to become an Artificer.

To be an apprentice in the Royal Navy means you must join up and I don't think any of us had any idea of what we were to face. At the age of sixteen we had to sign on for twelve years but that didn't begin until we were eighteen years old so in effect, we were to serve for fourteen years.

HMS Fisgard

Training began at HMS Fisgard in Torpoint in Cornwall, and we were met at North Road railway station in Plymouth by a Chief Gunnery Instructor with a truck to transport us to the camp at the beginning of September 1952.

LETTING OFF STEAM

Each of us was allocated to a hut with a bed and locker. We spent several days signing on, drawing our kit that was to be kept in the locker, every item had to be marked with your name, and how to display it for a kit inspection.

There were eight divisions with four huts to a division and my hut P7 was in Duncan division. The eight divisions were divided into an East and West configuration of four each side with a parade ground dividing the two and Duncan was on the West side. There were about thirty to a hut who were a mix of new entries and apprentices who had already served up to sixteen months.

The training course consisted of four years divided up into twelve terms numbered from 1 to 12 with each term being approximately four months long, so each hut contained individuals from 1 to 4 classes for training at Fisgard and only lasted for four terms.

> *... there was a fagging system at Fisgard, similar to that at public schools, which meant us new entries (Sprogs) had to 'fag' for the boys in the senior class in 4 class.*

The training at Fisgard gave an insight into the five disciplines of Artificers in the Navy; Aircraft, Electrical, Engine Room, Ordnance and Shipwright, and during that time we were assessed to see to which discipline we were best suited and also gave us an idea which we would prefer.

Artificer is the Navy's title for a skilled artisan after Tubal Cain, the Artificer in the Bible (Genesis 4:22)

Once we were allocated a trade, we would be transferred to a different training establishment. After Passing Out from twelve class we were allocated a depot within the Royal Navy where we would complete the fifth year, usually on a ship at sea although Aircraft Artificers could end up on an air station.

Something new to me was that there was a fagging system at Fisgard, similar to that at public schools, which meant us new entries (Sprogs) had to 'fag' for the boys in the senior class in 4 class. It was of course illegal, and the authorities knew about it but were powerless to prevent it. I remember little of it and can't remember the individual for whom I was a fag. Similarly, I have forgotten who had to perform as a fag for me when I reached the dizzy heights of the senior class. It was also a time for making new friends and some of those friendships have lasted until this day, but others are no longer with us.

Terms

Our first term consisted of woodwork and not something at which I excelled. Even so I managed to pass the practical examination and entered the second term, a venture into working with iron and steel.

This was a lot more difficult and sometimes painful! We had to learn how to cut the metal with a hacksaw, a hammer and chisel and various files. There were a lot of bloodied hands where the chisel was missed by a swinging two-pound hammer until we managed to gain an element of accuracy. The final test in 2 class was to fit a mild steel block 2 inches long by 1 inch square into a cast iron block 4 inches square by 1 inch thick with a tolerance of 2 thousandths of an inch or less, from rough metal using the tools described.

This was to be achieved without the use of a micrometer but just a steel rule and callipers. We were given 40 hours to complete this which brought a smile a few years later when something very similar was included in our final test job and was completed in a little over an hour!

The third term was a mixture. We spent three weeks in the Tool Room learning about marking out and the instruments that were used to do it. Then to the Welding section for electric and gas welding followed by a couple of weeks working with nonferrous metals and the technique of Annealing and Braising on an open fire. The final thing was in the Engine Smithing Shop. Here we worked in pairs around our own forge, made our own tools and learned how to use large power hammers.

All of these instructions were to help us decide which branch of Artificer we wished to be and over the course of the three terms we were required to make a first and second choice. At the start I wanted to be an Electrical Artificer but that was soon changed to Ordnance to maintain weaponry and later I thought of being an Aircraft Artificer, all the changes brought about by the instruction we were given. I never gave a thought to being a Shipwright even though it involved more than woodwork.

So, at the end of 3 class I was told I would be trained as an Engine Room Artificer (ERA) and I had to choose whether to be a Fitter & Turner or an "Outside Trade" which would be as a Coppersmith or Boilermaker. Looking back now I think it was the best choice even though I didn't make it!

Term 4 and it was all machine tools. Lathes, milling machines, shapers, grinders etc. The great majority were lathes, belt powered from an overhead drive shaft driven by a large electric motor at the end of the line. I did get lucky as there were a few machines at the end of each line, which were independently self-powered, and I was allocated one of them. I loved working with machine tools and excelled at it.

I did not play football or rugby at HMS Fisgard. I don't remember why but maybe I wasn't good enough, but I used to enjoy doing the Assault course in competition with other divisions for fun, and even more so since I was one of the marksmen. This meant being in a team to negotiate various obstacles of ropes, nets, ditches (often flooded) and buildings as quickly as possible and shoot at several targets at the end. The Duncan team were very good at it, and I was also the Duncan rifle shooting captain.

Of course, over the four terms we had to do our drill on the parade ground but after five years at the RHS I did not need a lot of instruction about how to march and salute. Regularly every Sunday and on other occasions too, Divisions were held, and we had to fall in for inspection, march past and salute our captain. So, we passed out.

HMS Caledonia

Having passed out from HMS Fisgard as an ERA Fitter & Turner apprentice, I found myself in Rosyth in Scotland at HMS Caledonia along with all the other ERAs, Ordnance Artificers, and Shipwrights, the Electrical Artificers had gone to HMS Collingwood in Hampshire and the Aircraft Artificers to HMS Condor at Arbroath in Scotland.

Now I was a resident of Saint Vincent division but in company with a couple of friends from Duncan in Fisgard although others had been sent to different divisions. The fagging continued so now I had to fag for someone new.

The factory work was more intense now and school lessons more technical. In the factory I found myself at the fitting bench again for at least three terms and the nearest I would get to a machine tool was a pedestal drilling machine. I found work at the fitting bench somewhat challenging and spent a fair amount of my free time doing extra time (usually Saturday afternoon) in the factory.

Each job had a set time for it to be completed and any extra factory time was added to the normal instruction time and consequently the penalty for exceeding the set time meant that I did not get very good marks. Each job was a test of our ability and a pass mark of at least 40% was required on completion of it.

We were endeavouring to work to a tolerance of thousands of an inch, without the use of a micrometer and marks were deducted for every thousandth beyond the set measurement and I ended up with a lot of time penalties! At the end of 7 class (twelve months) we were assessed on our overall performance, and I must admit, mine was not good.

Failure meant taking 7 class again and a similar result after that was a discharge from the RN apprenticeship scheme and the Royal Navy. I was puzzled why I was not required to do 7 class again since I did not achieve the required standard, but I learned later in my training that the assessment board had the idea that I was trying to get thrown out of the Navy, so I was progressed into 8 class!!! Nothing was further from my mind.

Machine Tools

8 class and I was back among the lathes again. Extra factory was history and struggling to make 40% too. Each machine was independent, and the overhead belt driven lathes forgotten. Now my marks for each set job were always beyond 70% and I enjoyed everything about learning to be a Turner. Each job had various tests and it was fascinating finding out how to cut screw threads, square threads, acme threads, external and internal as well as multi-started and left and right-handed. I was fast too so there was no danger of time penalty points.

By the time we had reached 9 class we were considered good enough to help out the maintenance staff of Rosyth Dockyard and we started working on proper jobs. In one particular instance I had to machine the crosshead of a steam piston shaft that was being repaired, using a boring machine and I set up the machine to cut exactly as it had been marked out in the Tool Room only to find I had machined it 30 thousandths of an inch under size!

After that I found myself in the milling section and the steam piston shaft arrived there having been rebuilt up again and I made exactly the same mistake with it only this time it was 40 thousandths of an inch under size!! I have never machined down to the marks ever again as a first cut. At sea there is no spares shop "down the road" so our skills with the tools was necessary to manufacture our own spare parts whenever we needed them.

Now we had to learn other aspects of our trade as really working in the workshop was a minor part of the job at sea, so the tools were left behind. There were life-size mock ups of a complete engine room complete with High- and Low-pressure steam turbines although not operational. It was more a case of our becoming familiar with the size of various pieces of equipment and we could recognise what it was, and we had to learn how to strip down and rebuild every piece of equipment that we were likely to meet in a ship.

I also spent a couple of days aboard HMS/M Aurocks and HMS/M Tireless as part of my sea training, spending most of the time underwater. These two boats were operational and running from a depot ship (HMS Adamant) which was berthed about the same place as the one that was servicing my Dad's boat in Scotland. In 9 class too we did a basic course on the internal combustion engine since some vessels are powered by petrol or diesel engines.

By the time we reached 12 class we had not touched any tools for a couple of terms, and we returned to our lathes to prepare for our final test job and the final examination in the classroom.

The theory exams came first and in the first few weeks I became extremely antisocial whilst studying and swatting all the subjects as I was quite convinced, I was going to fail and have to do it all again. Even so, it must have paid off as my final result was a lot better than anything else I had achieved over the years. I was elated by this and spent a considerable amount of time with my friends celebrating.

This proved quite problematic as during this time we were taking part in our final test job (with a hangover!), and I was very confident of my ability to pass it and complete my training. As it happened, I and a couple of my friends, failed to attain the required pass mark and had to return to the establishment for one more month of the next term to do the test again. Probably the fitting side let me down again.

The final test job is usually a secret and the drawings for it are presented at the beginning of the time allowed for completion and the planning of the operation has to be included in the time allowed. I guess we were lucky that our repeat test was exactly the same as the test we had failed which cut planning down a little and we were all successful the second attempt!

There was the usual period of leave after we Passed Out from HMS Caledonia and I and three of my friends organised a get together in London for a celebration. Unfortunately, one of them broke his leg on the way home after passing out, and couldn't attend so we separated his contribution, and all three of us descended on his home to celebrate with him in his hometown of Tonbridge.

Afterwards I spent a weekend in London at the home of one of my dad's brothers, uncle Fred. My cousin Fay and I developed a great deal of affection for each other during that time.

Chapter 4

The Real Navy & Sea-going Ships

Training complete

Having successfully completed that part of our training, it was now time to go to my assigned depot as an Engine Room Artificer, Fitter & Turner, Fifth Class. I was now a Leading Hand and wore a badge of a single fouled anchor on my left sleeve with three other classmates, and as we were all the same rank using the simple process of my being the oldest of four, I was put in charge and given the necessary paperwork of three other Fifth Class ratings to travel by train from Rosyth to Devonport Barracks.

There is no direct route from Scotland to Plymouth and we were to go there via London. We had lots of waiting time between the connections necessary to make the trip and the longest wait was in London where one of the three lived and when we arrived there, he took his buddy home for breakfast with the promise that they would be in time to make our connection. I left the third rating to his own devices, to do something similar by visiting uncle Fred's family, and Fay!

When I returned to Waterloo station, I found the third rating loading our kit onto the train. Each one of us had a toolbox, a hammock, a full kitbag and a suitcase and Fay and I arrived in time to see him load the last of them into the train. The time came for the train to leave and there was no sign of the other two Fifths, so I had an unpleasant six-hour trip to Plymouth trying to think up an excuse about how I had lost them!

Fay met the two of them arriving just as the train left and helped them find a train that left Paddington station an hour after our train and arrived in Plymouth an hour before ours. They were waiting on the platform of North Road station when we arrived in Plymouth, and it was with great relief that all four of us got together to go to Devonport Barracks. I have forgotten how we got there with so much kit!

HMS Drake

It is said that as long as you have a piece of paper in your hand you can walk around barracks all day and not get questioned, while doing the joining/leaving routine and so I found myself doing the routine to join HMS Drake, Devonport Barracks. This involves visiting all the departments listed on the card you are given so you can be signed in and each department will rubber stamp the card. I think it took me three days to collect all the necessary stamps and I joined the Reserve Fleet! This was just the title of the maintenance department that was operated from barracks and a few days later I had to do it all again when I was sent to my first seagoing ship.

HMS Mounts Bay F627

An anti-submarine Bay class frigate, with main propulsion of two Triple expansion Reciprocating engines. All during our training we were instructed about steam turbines as a ship's main propulsion and that triple expansion reciprocating engines would be something we would be unlikely to see and here I was on a ship that had them! It turned out to be an advantage eventually as I gained valuable experience in this type of machinery that became useful in later life as a civilian although not of this size.

1957 and my first trip abroad as a working individual and we headed for the South Atlantic. We were lucky that the ship did not get diverted to the Suez crisis. Like most trips, first stop was Gibraltar and then on South along the West coast of Africa visiting various ports, Showing the Flag, including Accra for the independence celebrations of Ghana. We also called at St Helena where I was able to visit Longwood House, that Napoleon occupied during his exile and eventual death, and see the grave site. Our destination was Simonstown in South Africa, which was to be our base on the South Atlantic station.

During this time Fay and I carried on a quite prolific effort in letter writing but I was devastated when she told me that her father had told her to stop and there would be no further correspondence.

Apart from doing our job of maintaining the ships equipment, Engine Room Artificers are watchkeepers and supervise the running of the ship's machinery 24 hours per day. Consequently, we had our own mess separate from other senior ratings who were not watchkeepers, so we didn't disturb them during changes of watch.

All the ERAs on the Mounts Bay were Chief Petty Officers and I as a Leading Hand had the privilege of being accommodated in the ERAs mess. It was also a disadvantage in that there was no-one of my age in the mess with whom I could go ashore on leisure activities and the CERA (Chief ERA) did not like me associating with ratings of lower rank!

Obviously, my senior messmates did not want a twenty-year-old in company with them when they went ashore either although we did have some really good times. I spent my twenty-first birthday working under the ship while it was in Simonstown dry dock. Celebration came later!

We crossed the South Atlantic in atrocious weather, at times force 11 gales...

Our job of Showing the Flag and policing the South Atlantic continued with a tour of various ports along the South African coast and after leaving Simonstown, the first call was Port Elizabeth. Due to the hospitality of the South African people, this station is a favourite with the crews of RN vessels and lots of entertainment and sport is organised whenever a ship visits a port, and Port Elizabeth is known as the Friendly City and also, the Windy City!

The evening of the day of our arrival a dance was organised and although I did not consider myself to be much of a dancer, I went along. Did Fate take a hand as at that dance I met Valerie who was later to become my wife? The ship continued its tour to East London, Durban and then on to Quelimane in Mozambique before returning to Simonstown.

We crossed the South Atlantic in atrocious weather, at times force 11 gales, and transported the Royal Marine band with us to perform ceremonial duties for the C-in-C. One sergeant was violently seasick all the way and sat on the deck next to the engine room sky light to keep warm in all weathers for seventeen days!

On the way we looked in on Tristan da Cunha but that is hardly the place for a run ashore. Not my forte but there was excellent fishing for crayfish and snoek. We had a national serviceman as the messman of the ERA's mess who was an ex-fisherman from Scotland, and we made hoops for him to produce nets that could be hung over the side of the ship.

South America

First stop was Bahia Blanca, the Argentine naval base. I was particularly pleased that I did not go ashore there as Jolly Jack Tar had just experienced a stressful crossing and wanted to let his hair down. He certainly made an impression as approximately 50% of the ship's company ended up in gaol that first night! The next stop was Buenos Aires where I met a couple of old shipmates from training who were serving aboard HMS Warrior, the aircraft carrier that Argentina was buying from the UK. We continued up the river Plate to Fray Bentos in Uruguay. This place was constructed for the employees of the corned beef factory to live in, and they entertained us well.

Then on to Rio de Janeiro where a group of four of us hired a taxi for the day and asked the driver to "show us the city"! I particularly remember the ride along Copacabana Beach and up Corcovado to see the statue of Christ the Redeemer. The ship eventually completed her commission in Plymouth and my mother was part of the group of visitors to meet the ship.

HMS Royal Arthur

On return to the UK, I went home on leave and while there I was granted an extra few days. I did not understand the significance of this until I went back to my ship and found I had been drafted to the dreaded Petty Officers training establishment. I had to travel there with two Petty Officers and our van was searched before we left Devonport dockyard by the Dockyard Police.

I was extremely anxious as I had about 160 duty free cigarettes above my allowance and feared a charge of smuggling. As it happened my fears were somewhat pitiful as the other two POs had several thousand cigarettes in excess between them and were arrested! Having now missed my train I was returned to the ship where a lot of effort was applied to find an alternative train for me to proceed alone. I later found out that my two intended travel companions were busted down to Able Seamen!

The POs training course at HMS Royal Arthur was feared mainly by people who hadn't been there and their information about the place was based on stories they had heard about it. On the other hand, I found it to be some of the best times I have had in the Navy, maybe due to the company of my fellow trainees, and I think we earned the reputation of being one of the worst disciplined classes to pass through the establishment, BUT we sure had a lot of fun!!! At the end of the course, I was given a draft to HMS Centaur, an aircraft carrier.

Maybe it was for the best but to me it was a disappointment. A new development was that a rating could choose where he could be considered to next be serving and I had chosen to go to an aircraft carrier, but it wasn't what I really wanted.

Diesel power interested me much more than steam and I would have loved to go to one of the new diesel-powered frigates, but a big ship would have offered me better chances of promotion and instruction and the biggest were aircraft carriers.

The application form was completed by the Engineer Officer in consultation with me and when I left HMS Mounts Bay, he told me he had recommended me for a diesel frigate, but I guess it didn't carry as much weight as my choice.

Valerie arrived in the UK as I completed the Petty Officer training course and stayed with my mother until we were married later in the year.

HMS Centaur R06

Something I liked about the Service was that if your ship contained new equipment then we, as the people who had to maintain it, were sent on a course so that we had a thorough knowledge of it. HMS Centaur was in a complete refit and being fitted with the latest steam catapults and arrester gear so that it could handle the latest naval aircraft. Several of us were sent to HMS Daedalus for two weeks instruction on steam catapults and arrester gear and when we returned to the ship, we were able to witness the installation of all this equipment.

It was a long refit, and we spent several months getting to know our way around the carrier and testing the new equipment. There are a lot of decks on a carrier and a lot of piping with valves that need to be identified on each deck and machinery spaces with which we need to be familiar.

The ship had two propulsion machinery spaces containing two Boiler Rooms with two Admiralty pattern three drum superheat boilers in each, two Engine Rooms with High- and Low-pressure steam turbines producing 36,000 HP through the gearing in two Gear Rooms with the associated shafting for twin propellors.

Having been newly promoted to Acting Petty Officer 4th class, really, I was still under training and each promotion is preceded by an oral and practical examination to demonstrate that we were capable. Having already been examined aboard Mounts Bay, someone failed to record the result and my promotion was doubted on Centaur and I had to do it again.

This delayed my promotion time which was in October but was not carried out until January, although I received back pay for the rate to the proper date once promoted. Later during my service aboard Centaur this had a very large effect on my career.

Artificers get rapid promotion which is resented by other ratings as we become Chief Petty Officers at a very young age whereas other rates take much longer, and ERAs get promoted even faster than other Artificers too. All of this is dependent on passing the necessary exams to accept the responsibility that goes with the job. If you fail the exam, you don't get the promotion!

If an ERA was seen wearing Good Conduct badges, then he would be a rarity as Chief Petty Officers (CPO) don't display them, and they are only allocated after four years' service. As we had to sign on for twelve years from the age of sixteen our first Good Conduct badge would only be displayed at twenty-four after four years man's time, by which time we should be a CPO.

I was promoted to ERA3 (CPO) on 21st January 1960 aboard HMS Centaur in Singapore. That was the day that Centaur hit the jetty so hard that a lamppost some twenty metres away, sheared off and fell while I was Chief of the Watch in the 'A' Engine Room! The port side anchor was also broken and left high and dry on the jetty! I was promoted to ERA1 in April 1960 in accord with the directive of an Admiralty Fleet Order (AFO) 1206/60.

A motor fishing vessel (MFV) belonging to Devonport dockyard was loaned to Centaur so that officer cadets aboard could be trained in physical seamanship and navigation etc. while the ship was in refit, and I was given the job of being its engineer.

Naval discipline was maintained of course but it was good to get away from the routine of a big ship and this lasted several weeks. We visited villages along the Cornish coast, we paid a visit to Alderney in the Channel Islands and also St Marys in the Scilly Isles.

I had two diesel engines to maintain, one Lister four-cylinder two stroke for propulsion and a Lister two-cylinder four stroke as a generator and fire & bilge pump drive plus the usual equipment aboard the boat.

We were plagued by exhaust problems from the generator which seemed to baffle the dockyard engineers and was not satisfactorily repaired.

With another breakdown on the way to the Scilly Isles I got permission from the captain of the boat, a lieutenant, to modify the exhaust system and we had no further interruptions.

Eventually the refit was complete, and we spent the necessary time at the Portland base "working up". Every ship goes through this to get the ship into its best fighting condition with simulated incidents and exercises.

The problem with aircraft carriers is that they are run by naval officers and ratings from Fleet Air Arm bases who rarely go to sea! We, as the usual general-purpose sailors, were merely there to take the ship wherever it had to be to allow the airfield to operate its aircraft and everything in that line takes preference.

The work up continued during the winter north of Scotland doing cold weather trials. Being in charge of one of the flightdeck catapult crews I was dressed in some interesting layers of clothing. After my underwear I donned a sweater, followed by my boiler suit and another sweater, then my cold weather suit which was full of Kapok and other insulating material, and the foul weather suit made of waterproof material. This was finished off with heavy non-skid boots, sheepskin mittens and our departmental identification bib and hat.

In one sad incident when my opposite number was on watch, a Sea Venom that had just landed had a brake failure meaning the pilot lost steering control, collided with him knocking him as it went over the side and into the sea.

The ship could not stop as other aircraft were waiting to land and he was concerned that his heavy boots were going to drown him, so he decided to kick them off but changed his mind when he thought he would have to pay for them! I could not understand why someone would rather drown than pay for a pair of boots. He was rescued by the duty helicopter that flies during take-off and landing operations for this purpose, once all the aircraft had landed.

LETTING OFF STEAM

The pilot of the Sea Venom was not so lucky who was lost with the aircraft. The Leading Stoker of our crew was very seriously injured in the incident and had a leg removed in the ships operating theatre, and later the second leg also removed in a hospital in Lisbon.

We worked watch on, watch off, in twelve-hour watches. To prepare a catapult for operation three hours are required to warm it up and test it with an unloaded firing. Sometimes this had to be done just to launch a single aircraft and a similar amount of time was needed afterwards to shut it down, so a long watch!

HMS Centaur was required to serve a twelve-month commission in the far east and our first port of call was Copenhagen but now I was serving my time in the engine room instead of on the flight deck. From there we headed south with the usual call at Gibraltar after a visit to Lisbon, and on to Malta, where I was the driver of an MFV again but this time delivering members of the crew on "banyan" trips to various beaches.

> *... where I committed a very unusual offence and was charged with 'Prejudicing the position of the British Far East Fleet'!*

Through the Suez Canal into the Indian ocean, with a period in the Persian Gulf at Kuwait, stopping at Karachi, Trincomalee and arriving in Singapore. Here I sat the examination for my "Unit Ticket", the qualification needed to control a propulsion unit (boiler room, engine room, gear room, shaft tunnel and associated equipment) on an RN ship, and take full responsibility for it, with two of my shipmates and all three of us passed the examination. Now I was on the watch bill qualified to do the duties of a Chief-of-the-Watch although still ranked as a Petty Officer (ERA 4th Class).

After a refit in Singapore, we travelled to Hong Kong and on to Yokosuka in Japan. This was followed by a visit to Australia via another call to Hong Kong. First call was Brisbane where I committed a very unusual offence and was charged with *'Prejudicing the position of the British Far East Fleet'!*

I was the duty Chief-of-the-Watch on the morning that we sailed so I had to take the lighting up watch, and a junior ERA was allocated as my throttle watchkeeper who, unbeknown to me, had never been in the engine room before! I sent him to remove the turning gear, which is situated in the Gear Room but, in his ignorance, he removed the clutch from the HP turbine which connects it to the main gearing, in the Engine Room.

Had we continued lighting up with the machinery and applied steam to the turbines in this state, serious damage would have occurred and perhaps, loss of life including mine, and crippling the ship. The error was discovered, and everything was returned into the correct state before steam was applied, and the ship was able to sail on time.

Later I had to face the captain as one of the Captain's Defaulters and judged to be guilty. The punishment would at least have been loss of rate but I was carrying out Chief Petty Officers duties while I was a Petty Officer so I could not lose what I didn't have! I was given a Severe Reprimand, but it would not be recorded on my Service Certificate when I left the ship. Later the Engineering Commander (GOD to us!) explained to me that he did not consider loss of leave or pay (usual punishment) to be appropriate for a technical offence and had discussed it with the captain.

I had to suffer further punishment by being removed from the watch bill which meant I would be able to have a full night's sleep every night instead of getting up to go on watch at various times at night!!!

Meanwhile, the ship continued its tour of Australia, Christmas in Sydney, then on to Melbourne and Fremantle. Whomever was substituting me on the watch bill had complained enough for me to be reinstated and the ship continued back to Singapore via Sourabaya and the incident of the ship hitting the jetty. Later that day I was a member of the Captain's Requestmen when I was promoted to Chief Petty Officer ERA 3rd class.

Chapter 5

Return to the UK

Promotion

Having been promoted, I was given charge of the port catapult in the machinery space instead of on the flight deck, as a watchkeeper and taken off the Engine room watch bill. With only two of us I was now back to a twelve-hour watch instead of the four-hour engine room although a watch rarely lasted that long.

On the way we were involved in the usual exercises with ships of other nations and a visit to the Indian naval base at Cochin. On the way to Mombasa the ship was diverted to Gan in the Maldives to supply aviation fuel to the RAF who were running short! At least that is what we were told, but in all probability there was a political reason for It, and our support tanker would probably do a faster job of it. Another visit to the Persian Gulf and then a return through the Suez Canal with calls at Aden, Gibraltar, to our home port of Devonport and some welcome leave.

I requested a diesel frigate for my next draft and was eventually successful, but I would need to have a course of instruction on the Internal Combustion Engine and associated equipment before that and I ended up at HMS Sultan the establishment in Gosport. I was first in my class during the nine-week instruction and consequently I was recommended for a Charge job (Engineer Officer of a small ship) and diverted to the Napier Deltic course instead of the ASR1 diesel engines of the frigates.

The Deltic is a very interesting engine in use on Coastal Minesweepers, with 18 cylinders containing 36 pistons and 3 crankshafts for propulsion with an incredible acceleration rate, and a 9-cylinder 18 piston engine as a Pulse generator for minesweeping. Obviously, I was not earmarked for a position on one of these ships and a different draft had to be arranged for me and I was sent to HMS Drake to join the High Speed Target Towing Vessel (HSTTV) Squadron. I was now the Engineer Officer of HSTTV Gay Charger.

HSTTV Gay Charger P1047

This was an ex-MTB converted to towing duties, with three Packard V12, mechanically supercharged petrol engines, 1200 HP each, burning High Octane aviation fuel for propulsion, and a Vosper V8 petrol engine as a generator – a little boat with a lot of power! There was no armament, but a winch was mounted on the stern with a very long cable! It was a boring job in a way as all we had to do virtually every day as duty boat, was to patrol backwards and forwards along a course, four or five miles off the shore, as a radar target for the gunnery school at HMS Cambridge to track our passage.

> ... had the privilege of being one of the support boats for the first ever Daily Express International Offshore Powerboat Race from Cowes in the Isle of Wight to Torquay.

Occasionally we were required to be the stand-by crash boat for an aircraft doing similar duties for the gunnery school and would wait in Cawsands Bay all day at anchor, as rescue. We would only stream a target astern for the gunnery school to shoot if there were no other ships in sight, and this was taking place in the English Channel!!!

We would also do "Showing the Flag" duties by visiting small harbours along the coast and I was disappointed when our visit to Gloucester was cancelled as we were not allowed to travel up the River Severn at more than 5 knots and I would have enjoyed showing my relatives round my boat. Our minimum speed was 8 knots, on one engine!

Two boats were required to provide a guard of honour at the British Embassy in Paris for the Queen's birthday (1960) which made a fourteen-day break for us and an interesting and amusing experience travelling along the river Seine.

We also had the privilege of being one of the support boats for the first ever Daily Express International Offshore Powerboat Race from Cowes in the Isle of Wight to Torquay. My boat was on the slipway, so I had to stand-in for the engineer of Gay Fencer, who was on leave.

We were the ones who needed the support however as we staggered into Torquay on one engine, with the two others incapacitated (broken camshaft and damaged fuel pump), and a generator with a blown cylinder head gasket meaning we couldn't charge batteries – most annoying as I had spares on my own boat. All this took place in a Force 6 gale. I loved the job, but it came to an end soon after. Back in Devonport the two damaged engines were removed and replaced with brand new units.

I made a promise to my wife that if I was ever sent on another draft to the South Atlantic, then she could go back home to South Africa for a holiday during the ship's commission in those waters and our stay in Simonstown, the South African naval base as I was given my choice of a diesel-powered frigate. She got her wish when I received a draft to HMS Puma.

HMS Puma F34

I had to return to HMS Sultan for two weeks to do the specialist familiarisation with the ASR1 diesel engine that I should have done before. Puma had eight V16 ASR1s as propulsion and four straight sixes for power generation.

We carried a Chief Engine Room Artificer (CERA) and nine ERAs to maintain the equipment, one extra to control the spares. As one of the junior CPOs, I was one of the two to maintain four diesels and associated machinery for the Port unit, and a watchkeeper.

Every so often mess meetings are held in all ships, and at one of these another junior expressed a desire to change his "part of ship", quite a legitimate thing to do, and usually if there is more than one it was an easy adjustment for swaps to take place.

Unfortunately, nobody else wished to change and I was detailed to change places from the Port unit to Outside Machinery which involves just about everything outside of the Engine Rooms: The Galley, Laundry, Refrigeration, Air compressors, Steering Gear (Hydraulics) and Motorboats, etc.

It was disappointing as I had struck up a good understanding with my immediate superior, but in a way, I was probably lucky as sometime later a serious fault was found in the crankcase of one of the port engines, and every engine of that type, in every diesel frigate in the RN had to be inspected to find out just how far the fault existed. No longer being involved with the diesels, the extra work did not affect me!

With the prospect of having to finance accommodation in South Africa, I applied for permission to stop shaving as a means of preventing me from going ashore and spending money! Whilst a beard is growing, one is not allowed ashore for 30 days so that it doesn't appear to the public that the rating has just forgotten to shave, and I had my last full shave on 2nd April 1962, the day we left the UK.

My plan backfired. A fault developed with the stabilisers on the way to Gibraltar and we spent several weeks there for repairs in which time my beard achieved maturity and I was able to freely spend money again with runs ashore. I have not had a full shave ever since.

We made calls at Freetown, Lomé, St Helena, and Cape Town and arrived in Simonstown in June. We continued with visits to South African ports around the coast, Port Elizabeth, East London, Durban, and Quelimane in Mozambique. Then on to Diego Suarez in Madagascar where I crewed for the Navigating Officer in a dinghy race which we won (maybe they let us win!), and back to Simonstown via a visit to the island of Reunion.

I applied for Station leave which was granted and I bought a second-hand car to drive from Cape Town to Port Elizabeth to spend time with my wife, her mother and sister. That turned into quite an interesting two weeks which is covered in a separate story in Chapter 6.

After a maintenance period the ship went to Tristan da Cunha to investigate whether the island was habitable again after the volcanic eruption had subsided. The ship managed to "find" an uncharted rock, produced by the eruption, which did serious damage to the port screw, and the bottom of the ship, and we returned to Cape Town for repairs.

While in the dry dock the ship looked like a toy in a bath as the dock was built to service the RMS Queen Mary and RMS Queen Elizabeth during the WW2 years! The repairs were only temporary but after a new screw was fitted to the port shaft, we went to Gibraltar via St Helena, Ascension Island, Freetown, and Bathurst. We returned to South Africa after a month for Christmas.

The time came for the ship to return to the UK via the South American ports, and I suggested to my wife to book her passage on a ship back to the UK and I was given the news that **she had no intention of ever returning to Britain.** It was devastating news and I asked what would become of our marriage as I had several years left to fulfil my contract and could not guarantee another commission in the South Atlantic on another ship? **I was told the decision was to be mine!**

Crossing the South Atlantic we made another stop at Tristan da Cunha without mishap continuing to Buenos Aires in the Argentine, and on to Fray Bentos in Uruguay. Next stop Rio de Janeiro where we received a visit from Lord Mountbatten who was on a world tour. Homeward bound from Rio with a stop at Las Palmas in the Canary Islands.

There we met our relief, HMS Leopard, and I made a request to change ships so I could return to South Africa, but it was denied as the Captain considered there was insufficient time to complete the exchange with an ERA from Leopard.

So, we returned to the UK where I was met by my mother and grandfather. I particularly enjoyed showing the old man around my ship.

I decided to leave the Royal Navy and put in a request to purchase my discharge. ***In retrospect this was the worst decision I have ever made in my life!***

I gave up the career I loved to save my marriage, but it would probably have survived the two and a half years that I had left to serve to complete my contract. I could have had to serve two of those years on another ship which would have been anywhere in the world and would make no difference whether my wife was in the UK or South Africa.

I understood Val's position in that it could not be very pleasant living in a foreign country, married to a man who went away for extended periods quite frequently, and all her friends and relations were not immediately available during his absence. On the other hand, she was warned quite strongly, before she was actually married what life would be like being married to a sailor. It had always been my intention to sign on again to serve a further ten years.

Chapter 6

The joy of the Garden route

The route

It was a real surprise when I received another draft to the South Atlantic station on the diesel frigate "Puma", so preparations were made for my wife to spend the next twelve months with her mother and sister in Port Elizabeth.

Her voyage on the "Cape Town Castle" was over in a couple of weeks and much quicker than mine as a problem with the stabilisers was discovered when the ship arrived in Gibraltar, keeping it there for some five weeks instead of a couple of days!

In an effort to save money for the extra expense of having to find accommodation while the ship was in Simonstown, I had decided to grow a full set as soon as the ship sailed from Portsmouth to limit any runs ashore, but five weeks in Gib took care of any savings! Having sailed from the UK at the beginning of April, we eventually arrived in Cape Town a week or so into June.

After the process of showing the flag around the South African coastal towns, Madagascar and other Indian Ocean islands, we arrived back in Simonstown at the end of July, and I applied for some station leave.

We rented a flat in Lakeside and I thought that if we had a car, I could commute to the ship and save the train fare every day. South Africans drive on the same side of the road as the UK, so a search for a cheap, second-hand car, was made which would also avoid the cost of airfares if we were to travel to Port Elizabeth.

Following up ads in the local newspapers took us to places, which I am sure, were never meant for white people to tread under the laws of the South African government, but ignorance is bliss, and my wife was not familiar with this part of the country! After viewing some American produced gas guzzlers (I well remember the huge Oldsmobile which virtually needed a communication system to talk to passengers in the back!), we settled on a 1948 Morris 8 "Tin Lizzie" and I spent some time checking over the vehicle for its trip from Cape Town to Port Elizabeth.

During the ship's visit to East London and having visited the town before, I remembered there was very little entertainment here, so I hired a car to drive to Port Elizabeth. Little did I realise that I was to spend nineteen years of my life living and working here in the future!

After about 100 miles, the car developed a clicking sound that fluctuated with the speed of the car...

The day before I set out, I asked a barman in one of the hotels what the condition of the road would be like. I was not at all expecting the answer I got when he told me it was good because he thought it had been tarred all the way now! I hadn't even considered it would be anything else, but this was Africa and none of the roads were up to the standard they are today.

LETTING OFF STEAM

On the day of our departure, with around 500 miles ahead of us, a hurricane hit Cape Town and the prevailing winds meant that it was headed in the same direction as us! That also meant that we would get a helping hand and with all the facilities in the car working properly (the windscreen wiper was working!) we were quite happy to continue.

The road N2 from Cape Town to Port Elizabeth is known as The Garden Route but with weather conditions like these we were in no position to enjoy the scenery!

After about 100 miles, the car developed a clicking sound that fluctuated with the speed of the car, but we persevered onward. The noise seemed to increase whenever we were heading uphill but was not at all intrusive along the flat. Unfortunately, along this part of South Africa, there is a lot of going up and going down again and not a lot of level road, and this was taking its toll on whatever was making the noise.

The car eventually came to a standstill just short of the town of Heidelberg and I had the unpleasant task of getting out, in the torrential rain, to push the car to a place where we could get assistance. Almost immediately, along came a Mercedes and the driver indicated for me to get back in the car and with the use of the bumper over-riders, he pushed us all the way to a garage at the intersection.

There my worst fears were confirmed. The crown wheel in the differential had stripped a couple of teeth so no further progress was possible in Tin Lizzie! However, my thinking was that there must be spare parts available in breakers yards for a car as popular as this, so the garage owner agreed to look after the car while the two of us made further progress.

LETTING OFF STEAM

I had never done any hitchhiking and didn't particularly relish the thought of doing it for more than 300 miles at all, especially with a wife wearing high heels, plus several suitcases and in the pouring rain! Why do women need so many clothes? We figured that being 170 miles from Cape Town, other cars would need fuel, so we stood on the forecourt of the garage and waited – at least we were under cover. We got lucky quite quickly when the driver of a Ford Anglia agreed to take us, plus all the accoutrements, as far as Knysna. This was about 140 miles in the right direction and with the torrential rain still scything down, we were very grateful.

I shudder to think how we would have fared had our transport still been serviceable because the road was in a really dodgy state by this time with large chunks of it washed away. Being someone who knew the road well, our driver did an excellent job of getting through. We parted company on another forecourt in Knysna with our saviour refusing any sort of remuneration.

We waited unsuccessfully for another lift and after about two hours, decided to find a hotel and continue the journey tomorrow. My wife had bought a new suitcase before she left the UK that I was carrying as we walked through the rain to the hotel, and I suddenly found myself carrying a handle while the rest of the suitcase decided to take up permanent residence in Knysna! I suppose compressed cardboard is not the best material for use in heavy rain. We spent the evening trying to dry out clothes using my wife's hairdryer.

The next morning it had stopped raining and at breakfast, my wife thought she recognised one of the guests and went across to his table to speak to him. It turned out he was a travelling salesman from Port Elizabeth and as he knew my wife, he agreed to give us a lift but only as far as Plettenberg Bay. Once again, it was in the right direction even if it was only 20 miles, so we accepted.

I have forgotten the make of car, but it was a lot roomier than the Anglia so now we travelled in comfort. The turn off to Plettenberg Bay went by in a flash but I said nothing thinking we would be dropped off somewhere nearby.

As it happened, the next stop turned out to be at Storms River 60 miles later, where there is a road bridge built by Italian prisoners of war and a tearoom. Here I questioned our driver about the change of plan at Plettenberg Bay and he said sales were poor, so he had decided to go home early. It was a great relief to sit and enjoy the rest of the journey and we were delivered right to the door of my sister-in-law's home in Port Elizabeth. Once again the Good Samaritan refused any payment – just said he enjoyed having the company.

The recovery of Tin Lizzie

After my hitch-hiking trip from Cape Town in the pouring rain, there was little time for relaxation and it wasn't exactly how I had intended spending my station leave but with the car in an immobilised state in Heidelberg and me in Port Elizabeth, I had to set about collecting the parts required to make it serviceable again. It was a case of touring the local breakers yards to see what was available and I eventually found a replacement differential (at least, that is what I was told!) for a reasonable price but how was I going to get back to the car?

My sister-in-law's husband heard about some friends of his from Uitenhage who were going to Cape Town by car and were prepared to give me a lift, as long as I could get to a pick-up point by seven o'clock in the morning. My sister-in-law's husband was happy to take me to this point, seventeen miles out of town, on his way to work although it was in the opposite direction for him. Being totally ignorant of the delivery arrangements made on the telephone, and some of it in Afrikaans, I was thankful and happy to go along with them. This was the famous South African hospitality working in my favour.

The next morning I was taken to the required spot, a junction with the Cape road from Port Elizabeth, well before 0700 hours and waited with my duffle bag full of the spare part and a change of clothes. I didn't know if a mistake had been made but in retrospect, I wish that junction could have been the one where the road from Uitenhage met the Cape Road!

I patiently waited, in the African bush, for two hours for a vehicle that just did not show up. These were days long before the invention of the mobile phone and with Heidelberg the best part of 300 miles away and Port Elizabeth 17, I decided the best plan was to return to Port Elizabeth so, I started walking.

It is not unusual to find black people walking along the road in South Africa, but it is extremely rare to find white people doing it and the hitchhiker's thumb is treated with a great deal of suspicion and as a consequence, passing vehicles didn't even attempt to slow down!

It turned into a long walk, and I couldn't decide which was the most painful, my feet or shoulders, at the end of it. That duffle bag with the differential inside got heavier with every pace.

I only had a limited time to get back to the car, repair it, return to Port Elizabeth and then collect my wife and drive back to Simonstown - finding another lift became very urgent.

In those days in South Africa, there were no car transporters and new cars were delivered to dealers by driving them to their destination and the drive was considered to be the running in period. The speedometer was disconnected and when the car was sold, it registered zero mileage, no matter how far it had been driven. Most people were quite suspicious about the way the vehicle was driven prior to their purchase but were assured that it had been done in a controlled manner.

I was to discover just how accurate that statement was when I was offered a lift in one of these convoys, provided I did not travel in uniform. Some strings must have been pulled as these delivery companies were not supposed to carry any passengers, hence the request for no uniform.

At that time Port Elizabeth was the "Detroit" of South Africa with a lot of motor manufacturers and associated industries in the area. And so it was that I found myself as a passenger in a brand-new Ford Zodiac Mark 4, pretending to be a member of staff of the delivery company, in a convoy bound for Cape Town.

The cars at the front and rear of the convoy were equipped with tachographs with all the others having their speedometers disconnected. I began to wonder if we would ever get to Cape Town travelling at 30 miles per hour for the first 50 miles but of course, this was all part of the running in process. The speed was increased by stages as the distance was covered. We also stopped at regular intervals; I presume to check that all the vehicles were still there! Interested customers were shown the tachographs reading.

> *... when the first problem arose! With the two differentials lying side by side, it became quite apparent that the replacement had never been in the rear axle of a 1948 Morris 8!*

Since we made an early start, I had had visions of arriving at Heidelberg reasonably early in the day so that I could start work on the repair of Tin Lizzie but with the routine of the convoy, most of the day had disappeared by the time we got to Heidelberg and there was only time for me to make my presence known to the garage staff.

They very kindly gave me a lift into town so I could check in at probably the only hotel for the night in this small town and also arranged to collect me after breakfast the next morning.

I had no tools other than a few spanners and the local mechanic told me I could use whatever equipment I needed that was available in the workshop but unfortunately, he personally couldn't give me any assistance! Both half shafts and the differential had been removed when the cause of the transmission failure had been diagnosed and I set about giving the replacement diff. a thorough clean.

That was when the first problem arose! With the two differentials lying side by side, it became quite apparent that the replacement had never been in the rear axle of a

1948 Morris 8! Although they were of similar size and the same number of holes in the bolt circle, the holes were in a different position and the mechanic told me I would have to go back and change it for the correct one! I then had to explain to him that apart from that impossibility, if a similar occurrence happened at sea, there was no breakers yard "down the road" and I intended to make the replacement fit!

I guess I had a bit of luck in that the mounting flange and the bolt circle were the same size as the old one, so it was just a case of drilling new holes in the correct position. The crown wheel was slightly larger too and some easing was necessary in the rear axle mounting. After fitting the diff. into the housing, I said a prayer and shone my torch down the axle housing and was relieved to see the axle bearings located in the centre. The two half shafts fitted without any further problems and the car was soon standing back on its wheels.

All during this time I got the impression that the locals were of the opinion that only a miracle would put this vehicle back on the road! I asked the owner if I could take the car for a test drive before he gave me the bill and drove into town where I was allowed to clean up at the hotel. On the way, I met the mechanic returning to work after lunch and he appeared quite stunned to see Tin Lizzie actually travelling along the road under its own power and almost lost control of his car.

The South African hospitality was apparent when I went to pay the bill, as all I was charged was for a piece of gasket material and gear oil for the differential, mere pennies really. All I had to do now was drive back to Port

Elizabeth, so I filled the petrol tank and set off on the return trip.

It was about this time that I was reminded of Murphy's Law! Dealing in the second-hand car market has an element of risk about it especially at the cheaper end and with antiquated vehicles. I had travelled about 50 miles without mishap when the ignition light lit up. I was not well acquainted with auto-electrics, and I knew that this meant there was a problem with the battery charger but so what, I was still making good progress along the road and everything else was still working OK.

I stopped and checked that I still had a fan belt and all the wiring seemed to be in place and no evidence of smoke so I continued on my way even though the ignition light would not go out. I was to discover later that the dynamo had burnt out due to a faulty voltage regulator and there was nothing I could do about that. The car had a 6-volt electrical system and…an electric fuel pump! Soon after passing Mossel Bay, the engine died.

It didn't take long to find that the carburettor had no petrol in it although I had plenty of fuel and the problem was traced to the fuel pump. However, giving the pump a little tap produced a whirring sound and we were mobile again.

This made me very aware how valuable my battery was going to be seeing that I now had no method of charging it and the daylight was fading and any signs of civilisation were far distant. The saving grace of older vehicles is that the engine can be started without using the self-starter as they have a crank handle especially for this purpose. Progress continued fitfully with my having to use the crank handle occasionally after a tap on the fuel pump but at least we were getting closer to Port Elizabeth.

The drawback to this was that the bonnet had to be lifted and propped open to get access to the fuel pump and there were two bonnet catches, one each side, that were operated with a key. Opening the bonnet was not a problem but closing it stole valuable time while the engine was running and emptying the carburettor. I did try once to just close the bonnet without securing it with the key and ended up driving totally blind after the bonnet lid had blown up vertically, completely obscuring any vision through the windscreen!

As I approached Knysna, I began to think that I should seek help only to find that it was past knocking off time so there was nothing available. A little while after, it became necessary to switch on the headlights! Now the battery really was in trouble and with the extra strain, the stoppages of the fuel pump became much more frequent. I tried to minimise this as much as possible by driving without lights and only switching on if another vehicle approached. I suppose I got lucky, as there was very little traffic.

Just beyond the turn for Plettenberg Bay there are two enormous river passes, the Groot River and the Bloukrans. Both of these gorges have been bypassed with bridges on today's new roads, but they had to be negotiated, in the dark with no lights, an unreliable engine and brakes that left a lot to be desired! Maybe it was as well that I could not see the full effect of the sheer cliffs and twisting corners but going down both of them was a real boon even if getting back up the other side involved a lot more work.

LETTING OFF STEAM

I have since learned that it is not unknown for the local wildlife that patrols these gorges, to include animals such as leopards, and I feel I would have been somewhat reluctant to make those regular excursions to persuade the fuel pump to carry on working had I known at the time! To this day I have never seen a leopard in the wild, even with several trips to wildlife parks such as the Kruger National Park, as they are very secretive animals.

> *... get up to the maximum speed possible, no matter what the speed limit was before the bowl emptied and then hit the clutch and coast as far as possible.*

Having got through the latest tests, the road was relatively flat, and I arrived in Humansdorp around midnight feeling quite confident that I would soon be in Port Elizabeth despite the regular stops. I had to take on fuel and I was able to phone my wife to let her know where I was and would be there within the hour. It was only another 50 odd miles.

Strangely, the car never failed whenever there was light available! It always waited for the streetlights to be left far behind and any work in the engine bay had to be carried out, in the darkness of the African bush, with the aid of a torch. By now things had deteriorated to the level where I could only drive the distance of one carburettor bowl full of petrol and then it had to be filled again.

The routine would be to get up to the maximum speed possible, no matter what the speed limit was before the bowl emptied and then hit the clutch and coast as far as possible. On one of these occasions, I raced across the

Gamtoos river bridge in the darkness, knowing there was a sheer cliff face immediately in front on the other side. I had no idea which way to turn but did not want to give up the hard-earned speed and once again, I got lucky as going left turned out to be the right choice!

I had not reckoned on the Van Stadens Pass either which was to cause an enormous delay even though it was not as threatening as the previous two, but quite close to Port Elizabeth. I was once told that snakes slept on the road at night to gain warmth and every time I vacated the vehicle I would do an inspection with my torch before setting a foot outside! Having coasted to the bottom of the pass, the battery had just about given up the ghost and I was struggling to get fuel into the carburettor, but I knew that if I could get to the top of the pass, it would be a straight run in to Port Elizabeth. After all, I had walked most of it a few days previously!

I managed to get a fair way up the hill, more by pushing than driving, when a truck came along behind me and stopped to offer help. I was told they would give the car a push and the first guy out had only one leg and a crutch!

The tarpaulin on the back seemed to come alive after a bang on the side of the truck and out came several black labourers but it didn't take long for the decision that it was a waste of time and they had only pushed for a couple of minutes! I was given a lift to the suburb where my sister-in-law lived, and I refused to allow the noisy truck to be driven right up to the house and walked the last few hundred yards. The time was 3am!

Tin Lizzie was still some 20 miles out of town so later that day I set about finding a new dynamo for the vehicle and then caught a bus to the top of Van Stadens Pass, which was the terminus anyway. Terminus seems quite a flattering term because it is just the end of the route and there was nothing there other than plain bush and the bus just turns round and goes back to town. Where any passengers went from there I have no idea!

I started walking down the descent and was very surprised to find that I had actually managed to get the car within sight of the top of the pass. Really, I should have been surprised to find that it was actually still there and all in one piece, but it was probably too big a challenge for the indigenous population to steal it! I fitted the replacement dynamo and went through the starting process to get some power into the battery and completed the journey to Port Elizabeth.

It all sounds so easy now but how many times did I have to persuade the fuel pump to run and how far did each run get me? Sometimes it was several miles and others, a few hundred yards but every inch was gratefully accepted!

There was no amusement at the time, but over the years I have had a good laugh and amused others, relating the adventure of recovering that car. But there was still the challenge of getting back to my ship in Simonstown 500 miles away, using that car, which proved to be almost as exciting!

Having since lived in South Africa for twenty-five years, I have driven along the Garden Route many times, in good and bad weather, but none of them have been as interesting or as rough as my first venture.

The return to Simonstown

After my epic journey to Port Elizabeth and subsequent trip to recover the injured vehicle, Tin Lizzie was now in

Port Elizabeth, but I still had to get back to my ship in Simonstown. Strangely enough I was quite undaunted by the exploits of getting me and the car to Port Elizabeth and felt confident that there would be no problem going back – or at least, none that could not be overcome.

At the time it never occurred to me that, there was another reason for the dynamo to burn out other than the age of the vehicle. Now that a replacement had been found and fitted, the battery was being charged and all the electrics were working fine. There had been no further trouble from the transmission, and we had used the car to run about the city during the rest of our stay so there was no reason to suspect anything else could go wrong.

I allowed a couple of days to get back to the Cape, just in case, and my wife and I set off in good spirits. There was no problem getting through the Van Stadens Pass compared with the previous trip but once we reached the top, the diff. started to "sing" to me and a quick check underneath the car told me there was a shortage of oil. I don't know what had happened to it because I checked the level prior to setting out which proved to be OK. Here we were in the African bush and no garage, or anything else in sight and after all the work I had put in, I was not prepared to risk damaging the differential again, so we were stuck!

A few minutes later, a young, black boy turned up riding a bicycle, so I stopped him to ask the whereabouts of the nearest garage. It turned out to be just a couple of miles further ahead, but I didn't fancy walking there and back for a pint of gear oil.

I thought about giving the boy a Rand (two Rand to the Pound at that time) to go to the garage and get the oil for me but guessed I would not see the boy again! I persuaded him instead, to let me borrow his bike for the one Rand, and set off leaving my wife locked in the car. I was no stranger to bike riding as I used to ride into Guzz dockyard every day when the ship was in refit, but I had never ridden a bike like this one!

It was quite an art to get it to go in the direction that the handlebars were aiming it but I eventually mastered it by the time I had reached the garage.

The gear oil was put into a glass cool drink bottle, without a top to it, and I now had to carry it in one hand and try to control the bicycle to get back to the car. Several times, I feared for my safety, that of the bottle and the oil, but it survived the trip and the oil ended up in the diff. housing and the young boy got his Rand. We were mobile again.

And so, the journey continued without incident, until the ignition light lit up again! We still had to negotiate the Bloukrans and Groot River passes but this time it would be in daylight and the fuel pump was still behaving itself, but for how long?

It was quite an experience driving through those passes and I remember one particular hairpin bend in the Bloukrans where the road dropped 40 feet in the turn. A lot of articulated HGVs in South Africa used to tow an extra trailer and when driving through these passes, the second trailer had to be parked at the top before driving through, park the main trailer and then come back with the tractor to collect the additional vehicle. Of course, this is no longer necessary with the new bridges. The highest bungee jump in the world is claimed to be from the new Bloukrans bridge.

With sunset due I was in no mood to perform the same routine in the dark with the fuel pump that I had to employ during the recovery of the car, so we decided to seek accommodation before the lights were required. We had heard stories of the holiday resort of Plettenberg Bay, and we headed in that direction – after all, it was out of season so there should be plenty of room.

The Beacon Isle hotel today is a five-star hotel, and I am very pleased to say, it did not have that rating in 1962 when the two of us booked in, as we were in no position to afford it! In fact, my funds were so low by this time that I was not sure we could honour the bill at all, but I would have to worry about that the next day and just enjoy what was on offer. As it happened, we were treated to some whale watching while we had breakfast the next morning and it was a great relief to find I was able to pay the bill. Now we could afford no more mishaps, as the contents of my wallet were in dire straits!

With an early start I was hopeful that we could reach our destination without the need to switch on the headlights as we were now at the mercy of the battery and unable to maintain the charge. The journey continued with the same routine as before with intermittent stops to restart the fuel pump, using the crank-handle to start the engine to save the battery and the frequency increasing as we got closer to the Cape, but we made it to the flat in Lakeside.

With time left of my leave, another search for a replacement dynamo but this time the services of an auto electrician were included. This was when I was told that the voltage regulator was asking the 6-volt dynamo to provide a charge of 16 volts for the 6-volt battery! With the problem fixed, I was now able to commute between my flat in Lakeside and the ship in Simonstown.

The ship was due to sail for Tristan da Cunha and the South American states, so we dispensed with the flat and my wife returned (by air!) to her sister in Port Elizabeth. But what do I do with the car because I would still want to use it when we got back?

The visit to Tristan was to investigate whether it was safe for the islanders to return to what was left of their homes. Most of us in the mess had become friendly with a local senior citizen called George, so I decided to leave Tin Lizzie in his charge until we returned, not really knowing how trustworthy he was! All the time we were away, I became the subject of ridicule in the mess, considering what had already happened to the car, and the suggestion that George would turn up with what was left of it in a carrier bag or worse, when we returned! As it happened, the ship didn't go as far as planned!

Puma discovered an uncharted rock, the hard way, while visiting Tristan! This rock, presumably the product of the volcanic eruption and we were at anchor immediately above it, punched several holes into the bottom of the ship.

When the ship moved to a new anchorage, the rock also managed to tear a blade from the port screw and buckle the other two blades, witnessed by me on the Engine Control Room (ECR) rev. counter, being Chief of the Watch at the time!

Of course, we knew nothing of the damage to the hull of the ship, other than what information the divers had provided about the screw, and the Chief Stoker wanted to know who was pumping out bilges and leaving an oil slick astern. We had to return to Cape Town for repairs, using only the starboard shaft, as the South African Navy had a ship in the Simonstown dry dock.

The Sturrock dry dock in Cape Town is huge, built to accept the Queens, Elizabeth and Mary, and Puma looked like a toy boat in a bath, with room for a 60,000-ton tanker behind her, once the water had been pumped out. As the water level cleared the bottom of the ship, the damage became apparent as the contents of the double bottom fuel tanks continued to pour out!

The damage was eventually patched up after much negotiation between the local engineering company and the Admiralty, a new port screw fitted, and the ship despatched to Gibraltar for more substantial repairs.

When we eventually returned to South Africa George did indeed come aboard with bad news. He said the car had been stolen and he had reported it to the police where he lived in Muizenberg! I could hardly disagree with him but found it hard to believe.

Val came back and we stayed with George and Pauline his wife, as we no longer had the flat in Lakeside and one Sunday we were out walking when I spotted Tin Lizzie driving past us! We were not able to stop it but called in at Muizenberg police station to report the sighting. Nothing happened at the time, but I later heard that it was being driven by the owner who had reported it stolen several months before! I wondered if he had ever noticed the modifications I had carried out while it was in my possession. All my exploits with Tin Lizzie were while I was driving a stolen vehicle!

HMS Osprey

The preferential drafting got me posted to the shore base at Portland and I joined the Coastal Defences maintenance crew. After six months I paid the princely sum of £125 to leave the Royal Navy and found myself back at HMS Drake carrying out the discharge routine and became a civilian. During this time, I was advised that I would have to join the Reserve List and then, as I would be living in South Africa, I would have to join the Reserve Special List!

Chapter 7

Emigration

Unemployed

Walking out of the gate of HMS Drake it occurred to me that all my security had disappeared for the moment as I had decided nothing about the future other than Emigration.

I had applied to join The 1820 Settlers Association which was a group assisting people who had applied to go to South Africa, to find work and accommodation as well as providing a discounted sea passage. I paid £22.00 for a fourteen-day sea trip to Cape Town from Liverpool aboard the RMS Empress of Britain.

The ship docked on 19th December 1963 and a two-day train journey on South African Railways to Port Elizabeth was not the best train journey I have ever had. I was met by my wife Val, and we took up temporary accommodation in the home of her sister's husband and family. It was Christmas time.

I told my wife that although I had joined her in South Africa I did not intend to die there, and I would eventually return to the UK. We took up residence in a one roomed flat on the third floor of a three-story building close to the centre of the city of Port Elizabeth once the festive season was over.

When I left the UK, I had packed all our household possessions into several packing cases and suitcases. The packing cases were very securely closed, and all the suitcases were locked, and I was asked for the keys before

I left Cape Town by the Customs officials since I would not be present during the inspection.

Everything was delivered to our new home free of charge but in a very different state to the one I had set up. All the packing cases had had their lids forcibly removed, but not replaced, with the contents on display, and the suitcases were locked but the keys were not included! I was very surprised to find that nothing was missing. I did not have spare keys to the suitcases, so I removed the hinge pin from the locks on each one to gain access without causing damage.

Employment

I had declared my skill as a tradesman to be a Fitter & Turner, but I had not used any machine tools since completing my apprenticeship, so I was not particularly pleased to find I had been allocated employment in a machine shop. I had not been personally interviewed regarding my employment in South Africa, and being attached to a lathe or milling machine was not how I fancied my future even though I was capable of this kind of work.

Having served on the MTB with V12 petrol engines, a frigate with V16 diesel engines, and maintained smaller minesweepers, all powered by diesel engines I was much more interested in that sort of line. I was eventually offered a job with the local Leyland agent as a motor mechanic. I am not a motor mechanic, and it was not what I wanted to do but there was nothing else in that kind of work in Port Elizabeth, or at least, it was not being offered to me.

All these opportunities being offered through the 1820 Settlers Association. Strangely enough, although I had a lot of experience, I was never given a diesel engine powered vehicle to maintain or repair during the whole of my twelve months service with the Leyland agent RL Weir.

RL Weir Ltd

The Rover manufacturing company was based in Port Elizabeth and the Leyland agent, RL Weir Ltd, was responsible for the pre-delivery service of every Land Rover manufactured there.

With the terrorist war taking place on the South African border, the South African Defence Force was ordering lots of Land Rovers for use in the army. In my twelve months there I must have carried out the service for at least two hundred brand new Land Rovers!

> *... I became a father when Rory was born. I was overjoyed to have a son and took an unapproved day off!*

Since there was little alternative work available, I decided to stay with the Leyland company for the full year to obtain my allocation of holiday, also learning about other aspects of motor vehicles, and then search for some different kind of employment.

In September I became a father when Rory was born. I was overjoyed to have a son and took an unapproved day off! My life was to change though and become one of extreme patience for me.

Long before we met, Val had decided that her two children were to be named Rory, and the girl would be called Kerry. I wasn't allowed any input as far as the names were concerned but I didn't object, and I didn't find them unattractive anyway.

There was a change however, once Rory was born when Val announced that there would be no more children! There was no discussion, just a unilateral declaration, and initially I took it to be a natural reaction after a first-time pregnancy and birth, which would pass with time.

As a very staunch Roman Catholic she intended to follow the strict rules of her church, and as a result I no longer had a proper wife, just a housekeeper. Since the use of contraceptives were not allowed, the only solution for her was no intimate contact at all. In time I did consider separation and divorce, but I had given up a life I loved in order to save this marriage and was now in a country where I had committed my future. Returning to the UK would not resurrect what I had before and was not allowed anyway as residence of a minimum of two years was required or full payment of the fare of transport to South Africa.

Port Elizabeth

There is a thriving harbour in Port Elizabeth and the idea crossed my mind that there could be my kind of work with one of the companies there. I did not particularly want to go to sea despite my history, but I was sure I could find something, maybe as maintenance back up.

I also wrote to The Globe Engineering Works (ship repairers) in Cape Town, asking if there was a position for me, even if it meant moving to Cape Town. As a result of that letter, I was invited to an interview with their Chief Engineer who would fly to Port Elizabeth to carry out the interview. When leaving the RN, individuals are supplied with documents that explain their capabilities to prospective employers, so armed with these documents, I went to a company called Irvin & Johnson for the interview.

It is a trawler company, and they supply South Africa on a par with Birds Eye in the UK. The engineer was very impressed with my interview and then told me that there was no vacancy available at the time. However, I was also told that with experience like this, he was not going to allow me to walk out of the door and would create a job for me until a vacancy became available!

Instead of maintaining trawlers, I was offered the job of motor mechanic for the company's fleet of vehicles which were normally covered by local garages! Not what I wanted at all, but with the promise of being part of the base staff for the trawlers when the opportunity presented itself, I accepted it, even though it was poorly paid.

Irvin & Johnson

While I was working for the Leyland agent, I was told it was possible I would be required to drive an HGV and when I exchanged my British driving license for a South African one, I was asked by the official if I wanted an HGV one, which of course I did! No test necessary, it was just an exchange.

I turned up for work at 07:00 and found that all the vehicles disappeared from the garage in a matter of minutes except for a 7 ton Austin van with no cylinder head, and a forked lift truck. My black assistant told me that the forked lift truck wouldn't go despite the efforts of various people, so it wasn't used! Nobody allocated me any work, and I could not see the forked lift truck standing there and not examine it, and by lunchtime it was chugging about the garage quite happily. Word must have got around inside the factory because I never saw it again!!!

The cylinder head for the 7 tonner was returned and fitted by the local agent with no input from me a few days later and seeing I had never driven an HGV I decided to have some practice by driving around inside the docks. The workshop foreman asked if I had an HGV license during a tea break and thinking he had seen me driving I assured him that I had. "Good," he replied," the management want you to drive the 7 tonner to Jeffreys Bay (approx. 50 miles away) to collect a load of fish tomorrow morning".

This turned out to be quite straightforward and became a regular pleasure jaunt really as I was required to do it every Friday morning. It was a break from the boring garage, and all I had to do was drive, loading and unloading was carried out by black staff at each end. Unfortunately, it came to an end when the workshop foreman complained to management that he did not agree with using skilled staff as truck drivers!

The next time it went out, without me, it broke down, and there was "panic stations" to get me to the truck, stranded with a load of fish in an unrefrigerated vehicle, as quickly as possible. I was given the manager's Vauxhall Velox and drove at over 100 mph for the first time in my life and collected a ticket from the National Traffic Police! I argued with management that if I hadn't been placed in that position, I would never have incurred the fine and eventually they agreed to pay it, but I had to drive some considerable distance to pay it as it could not be paid in Port Elizabeth.

A report came in that the truck that delivered fish to Uitenhage had broken down and would need to be towed back to Port Elizabeth. As far as we knew this was a refrigerated van of about three tonnes and would need more than my pick-up truck to bring it back, so a towbar was constructed and off I set in the 7 ton truck.

On arrival in Uitenhage, I found a minivan with a big hole in the sump! If I could have got it up to a higher level, I could have put the mini inside the 7 tonner, but I had to tow it instead and I could have done it easier with the pick-up! A workshop manual was purchased and during the next couple of weeks I had to strip and rebuild the mini engine and gearbox.

I had a disagreement with the workshop foreman when I refused to work overtime. He was never on time in the morning but was waiting for me when I arrived at my usual time of 07:00 the next day! He demanded that I resign since I did not work overtime the previous evening, so I obliged him and presented a letter to management. The two of us were called to the manager's office and I was given a lecture on the necessity of overtime working in the fisheries industry and asked to withdraw the letter! I explained that I would happily work necessary overtime but would prefer to be asked rather than ordered, since my previously delivered orders had come from people with gold braid rings on their sleeves. I was asked to work overtime the same evening and complied but when I turned up in the trawler engine room, I wasn't given any work to do and spent a paid hour doing nothing!

The vacancy I had been promised arrived soon after the overtime incident, and I was offered the job of maintaining the trawlers. I was happy to accept it providing the difference in salary came with the job, but apparently as it was the wrong time of year, this was not the case!!! Increases in salary only occurred in June, so I wrote another letter of resignation and went looking for another job.

Chapter 8

The Construction Industry

General Engineering

I found work very quickly as a fitter with a small construction company which was a subsidiary of a larger manufacturing company in Port Elizabeth. The work was extremely varied and interesting being something new to me.

Most of the work involved installing pipework on construction sites and I was at a slight disadvantage in that I had never been asked to carry out arc welding other than a few hours of my apprenticeship. In some cases, it meant I had to be accompanied by a welder whenever the job required that kind of construction. I was determined to correct this issue and set out to find out how to weld, steel pipework in particular, by picking the brains of the welders who came with me and practicing what I found out. Over a period of years in the construction industry, I became a first-class welder in both arc and gas welding.

As we were part of a larger company the work was not confined to Port Elizabeth, and I found myself on a contract in Johannesburg. I was not impressed with the design of part of this particular job. All we were doing was assembling machinery that had been designed and manufactured by the parent company in Port Elizabeth and an overhead conveyor collapsed because of poor design and materials.

A colleague and I manufactured a complete conveyor system, in situ, using more substantial materials over a period of days, and later we worked through the night and following day, removing the old system, and installing our new one! It was a much better conveyor that worked.

This was not the only time the design issue cropped up. It was probably due to cost cutting when tendering for work that certain items were omitted in the construction causing things to fail. Several vertical conveyors were installed in various supermarkets and department stores and these lacked stability, so there was a regular supply of breakdowns due to missing (cost saved) parts! I gained a reputation as the fitter who could solve the problem, with my employer and customer's staff.

This could not last and as a result the subsidiary companies were closed, and I was transferred to the parent company as a maintenance fitter. I was told there were only three Broom & Wade air compressors of a particular type in South Africa and this company had two of them! They were used to supply compressed air to the complete factory alternately, with the other on standby. I was given the job of completely overhauling one of these big machines, refitting white metal bearings etc.by 'taking leads', and scraping them to fit. It took about 2 weeks and on completion it was made the duty machine. After 24 hours successful operation, I was made redundant in preference to one ex-bus-driver-cum-fitter and one ex-barber-cum-fitter! I suppose as the most expensive qualified fitter on the books a saving in salary, and after approx. 3 years, I was job hunting again and the company closed permanently!

Albert Vaux & Co (Pty) Ltd

I found a replacement company by 'knocking on doors', which did similar work. Albert Vaux & Co (Pty) Ltd was a subsidiary of Bestobell Ltd and did the construction work for them. I was not happy having to go back to basics as far as salary was concerned but I needed an income and thought this would suffice until I could find something better. Little did I realise that I would work for this company for more than twelve years!

We were also hired out to assist industry where help was required. My first job was to instal two small fuel transfer pumps at a glassworks company and then join the rest of the crew on hire at the same glassworks. One particular job was quite amusing in that I was taken to a large room at the glassworks where there were a large number of constructed items lying in a pile in the middle of the floor.

I was told it was a frosting machine for plain light bulbs and needed putting together. I asked for the drawings and was told there were none available, but they would try to find some photographs so that I could see what the finished article looked like! The pictures never materialised but I was not put under any pressure to construct it quickly, and the odd visitor who had worked with the complete article was able to offer advice.

> *... not a good time for me, the two Mrs Deacons did not get on well together, and I was in in the middle.*

The main line of this company was that they were Steam and Heating Engineers, and the rest of the workshop staff were plain construction workers and knew little about steam in particular. The pipework that carries steam is just a little different to other commodities in that it continually moves during operation and cannot be bolted down. There were industrial boiler and steam plant installations plus the associated steam network and although I didn't have to do installation work in the RN, my past experience was quite useful. We did installation work for the two main boiler manufacturers in South Africa at the time, John Thompson Africa, and Babcock, handling machinery up to 50 tonnes deadweight.

My mother came to South Africa to see her three-year old grandson, Rory. This was not a good time for me, the two Mrs Deacons did not get on well together, and I was in in the middle. This was to do with a misunderstanding while Val was in the UK (we never did find out the cause) and was probably the foundation of why she had decided to remain in South Africa when I asked her to return.

My mother had booked a three-month holiday, but due to the dissention I asked her to leave and booked a return flight for her. Her reaction was to cancel the booking and left immediately for new accommodation! Things were a little quieter after that.

Port Elizabeth was 'Motor City' in South Africa at the time and big manufacturers like General Motors and Ford, were prominent employers and I have already mentioned The Rover company. Also, tyre companies, Firestone, Dunlop, General Tyre. Good Year Tyre, and Volkswagen were situated in the nearby town of Uitenhage. All these companies had large boiler installations so there was plenty of maintenance work and new installations. Other big steam users were the Wine & Spirits industry,

Stellenbosch Farmers Winery, and Distillers Corporation. Cadburys were also present, and I ended up working in all of these companies, sometimes on a particular contract or on hire to assist with labour.

In 1968 Port Elizabeth was hit with a violent storm. I didn't realise that heavy rain and flood water could cause so much severe damage although I am well aware of the power of water. 500 mm of rain fell in four hours. I suppose the familiarity of living in a particular spot for year upon year, maybe all their life, people do not comprehend that their home has been built in what was once a riverbed, and the river returns when floods arrive.

There were some amusing incidents. In the suburb of Newton Park, Cape Road, the main road was flooded but the traffic lights were still working, and some people were obeying the red and green lights while paddling canoes and small boats!

Even though the city is on the coast, most of it is on high ground and even a lot of that suffered flooding and the industrial part suffered quite severely at the lower level. I think our company must have made a great deal of money over a period of a few months as most of us were on hire to help with the recovery. I particularly remember working for a wire extruding company where there were hundreds of electric motors, all at ground level, and the floodwater only rose about 2 feet, which was sufficient to cover every motor! I spent 6 weeks removing, stripping them down to be dried out, and then reassembling them and putting them back in place.

Friendships

Soon after joining the company, I met Terry Wadsworth, another Englishman, 3 years younger than me, who had served in the Royal Artillery as a Bombardier, and we developed a friendship. He had planned to follow his father and become a Paratrooper (Red Beret) but due to a misunderstanding, he failed the course, at least that is the story told by Terry!

I suppose it was a case of opposites attract as Terry was a staunch Union man and I was not. Maybe it was just the comradeship of fellow tradesmen, yet we were so different in just about everything, and I often wondered why we became friends, but it lasted for many years, and for Terry, the rest of his life. According to Terry, a good deal of his life had been spent in nefarious activities, including working for the Kray twins in London, before he emigrated to South Africa.

> *... a rather aggressive Hungarian had joined the company, and it didn't take a lot to upset him! This was my introduction to Istvan Lajvort! We called him Steve.*

I find it quite intriguing that the lighter an object weighs, the heavier the machinery needed to produce it. We had a contract to install steam and water pipework in a paper mill and Terry and I were included as part of the crew to erect it. It was going to be a long contract taking several months to complete. Nearing the end, Terry was transferred to East London to continue a contract we had to install the steam network in a new hospital, which was losing money. Funny really, as Terry knew nothing about steam, and at about the same time I took some time off for leave.

When I returned, I was warned by some colleagues that I should "watch my step" as a rather aggressive Hungarian had joined the company, and it didn't take a lot to upset him! This was my introduction to Istvan Lajvort! We called him Steve.

He was a year younger than me, a Hungarian refugee, and had been in South Africa from the age of 16. When he arrived in the country, he could speak Hungarian and Russian but no other language. He spent his early South African life in Johannesburg and worked on the gold mines. I learned to respect this man as by the time I met him he could communicate in English and Afrikaans and also with the Indigenous people in Fanagalo, a language of the black people on the mines.

He enjoyed "helping" me with my daily newspaper crossword puzzle, a way of broadening his vocabulary. He was the strongest man I have ever met outside of a circus, he could also be very generous and gentle, and I never felt that I should "watch my step" while I was in his company. Terry and Steve were two of the greatest friends I have ever had.

Terry used to complain to Eric Rix our manager, that he needed help in East London because the amount of work he had was escalating and he was finding it difficult to maintain his presence on the hospital contract, which was a conditional clause.

Unbeknown to me he asked specifically for me to join him, and when I was offered the transfer, I refused as my feelings for East London have already been made public! Steve was sent in my place! This did not go down well with Terry, and there were times when the two of them were at loggerheads although they never actually came to blows, but both of them were of the opinion that any problem could be resolved by using fists!

Six months passed, and Terry was complaining again about the amount of work that was building up and a third tradesman was required in East London, preferably Jeff Deacon! This time I was told and reassured that it would be a temporary transfer until the hospital contract was finished when I could come back to Port Elizabeth.

I agreed and was to be the permanent fitter on the hospital contract, but I could work overtime after 17:00 each day and on weekends, if I wanted it. So, as a family we moved to East London, much against my wife's wishes. At the time I was working alone on a contract installing two new boilers and a completely new steam main in the private hospital where Rory had been born, and I suppose Eric considered it was far enough advanced for someone else to take over.

My first day at school in Dunoon, Scotland, 1940

Me with Thelma outside the front gate of the Barker house, 1942

Grampy. This old man lovingly took the place of my father until I went to South Africa.

Normal summer working gear, 1948

LETTING OFF STEAM

Back home after the commission on HMS Centaur, 1960

Promoted to Chief Petty Officer in Singapore, 21st January 1960

1961 – The crew of Gay Charger. We're all dressed up for a photo shoot in Plymouth Sound.

1953 – Aged 17 ½ and I had just received an increase in pay after first year of apprenticeship

1962 – Passport photograph before I grew my set

LETTING OFF STEAM

Mid Summers Day in 1958; my wedding day in Ross-on-Wye

1978 – A portrait I painted of Bullitt, my lovable companion

1980 – About to leave home to judge at a championship obedience dog show in East London

1982 – Settled with Fay in our home in South Africa

LETTING OFF STEAM

2000 – All dressed up for Colin and Julie's wedding

2001 – Fay, the love of my life

2013 - Steve Lajvort when I visited him on one of my tours

2013 – Terry Wadsworth when I visited him on one of my tours

2015 - Touring the South African game reserves

Chapter 9

East London

House hunting

The three of us established a reputation that there was nothing we could not do in the engineering world in the area, with Terry working as the Foreman/Charge Hand, and very soon we had too much work again, but staff levels were not increased. Eric Rix used to visit us every 6-8 weeks to inspect working contracts and search for new work. We even took over contracts that other competitive engineering works could not handle.

A year after moving to East London the town was hit by a storm similar to the one that had struck Port Elizabeth, and we were flooded out while living in a ground floor flat. This time I was committed to the hospital site so I could not be hired out as labour to local industry. Our flat overlooked a private sports club that had a nine-hole golf course attached to it and the entire premises became a raging river. After the flood we needed to completely refurnish the flat.

About this time, I bought my first new car. I traded in my old Opel Caravan which had served me well for six years, for a Renault 10, probably the worst car I have ever owned! It was a very comfortable car and rivalled more expensive vehicles in that department, but at the first service one year later, I was told the engine was worn out! I had doted on this car, nursed it, never thrashed it, and it came as quite a shock to be told this by the garage manager. I wrote to Renault explaining the circumstances and asked for an opinion why this should happen, although I had my own idea, but the reply told me the car was out of warranty and they would not offer any financial assistance, not that I had asked for any, or any opinion. Within days I traded it in for a Datsun 1200 saloon which gave me five years much better service.

Years later Eric Rix explained to me that the original quotation for the steam installation at the hospital had been estimated to last eight months but one of the conditions was that there had to be a working fitter on the site every working day. Unfortunately, the civil side of the contract did not go at all well, and there were numerous times when there was no wall on which to hang our steam pipes, but I had to stay on site with nothing to do and get paid for it! The contract was eventually completed after ten years, and I had to remain present right to the end. It did not have to be me of course, but all the extra retention on site had to be costed and Eric made a real killing for the company. By this time both Terry and Steve had left the company, and I was the sole artisan and I had been an East London resident for more than 6 years.

All my working life I have lived in rented properties, usually flats or apartments. Always on the move when I was serving in the Royal Navy, between various ships and bases, and after marriage we didn't think about buying a house at the time. I made myself a promise that if ever we did end up living in a house with a garden, then I would purchase a dog.

We rented a house in the suburb of Cambridge, so I immediately searched for a pup. I wanted a fair size dog with as little maintenance as necessary, so a short coat with little grooming. A Doberman litter filled the criteria and was advertised in King Williams Town, about thirty-five miles away, so Rory aged 9, and I went to have a look. How do you choose from a litter of ten individual pups that all look the same? The problem was solved when one of the pups chose Rory, so that was the one.

The only way Val would allow us to have a dog was that the dog had to live outside and not in the house, although I did not agree with the principle, if that was the only way I could have one, then I agreed. Once at home the pup spent most of the day on Val's lap, and when bedtime arrived, I went to put the pup outside, but Val objected quite strongly! My comment, "If it doesn't go out tonight, then it stays inside every night!". 'Bullitt' spent the rest of his life inside, to my mind the proper place for a dog! I did not realise the effect of owning this dog would have on the rest of my life.

Dog training

The Border German Shepherd Dog Club & All Breeds Training School was the only club that taught obedience training at the time in East London, and I knew that the Doberman had a reputation as a police and guard dog and could be quite dangerous if not trained properly, so I enrolled Bullitt and me.

Bullitt was now 7 months old, and quite a handful, and being with other dogs was real fun for him! I learned that it pays to start training as early as possible, and it took a long, long time to get through to him that he wasn't just there to play, even though it was included, but when he was released from the lead he would run amok and interfere with other classes.

Hence, all training should take place with the dog on a six-foot lead and slip-chain, so that commands can be enforced and backed up. It took just over a year to get real control of him, and we won two first prizes at the annual Championship dog shows for Obedience on his second birthday. Due to my persistence, I was invited to become a teacher in the club, and a committee member, and all I had to do was apply what the club had taught me.

Although I taught obedience training, I found it too rigid to enjoy it in competition as a competitor, and discovered there was Working Trials which involved a man and his dog working together in the Bush as a team, and a much more relaxed discipline.

By the same token, since I taught, I was encouraged to become a judge, and apply Kennel Union of South Africa (KUSA) rules in the competition ring. One has to serve an 'apprenticeship' for judging at local shows, writing a report, and following it up with a successful Championship show at each level of obedience standard. I passed all the levels except the senior Championship test. I had completed the local show examinations at this level and was due to judge at a Championship show when I left the country to return to Britain.

Competitors used to travel all over South Africa to enter Championship shows (three qualifications at different Championship shows and judges are required to create an Obedience Champion) and learned which shows to avoid after reading the schedule of judges for each standard. There were people that avoided shows if my name was on the list purely because I insisted on applying one test in a particular way, within the rules as I read them. A judge's main fear is that none of the dogs are able to successfully complete the test that has been set, meaning it is too difficult, but if one dog completes the test, they can relax!

I always had at least one! My last two Championship shows were held in Grahamstown in 1988.

The club had a Demonstration team, and we would perform at various events to show what can be achieved from training and as an attraction for new members. The dogs would perform basic control plus extras such as scent discrimination, jumping through flaming hoops, and detaining a "criminal" running away, and later children were invited to pet the same dogs to demonstrate their even nature as household pets. Julie's Golden Retriever, Tuppence, was a great favourite when she refused food that I offered her even though she lived in the same house.

Hobbies

I have always been good at sketching although not creative. My sketches were always copied from another source, like Disney, or magazines and comics. I remember one particular instance at boarding school when I copied the figure of a young woman in a bikini from a magazine and my drawing was confiscated by one of the masters, but I was allowed to keep the magazine! I suppose it was part of the draconian rules that governed our lives.

The dog club became quite a useful market with captive customers!

I didn't venture into colour until I was much older. The husband of my sister-in-law was given an oil painting by a well-known South African artist, and having seen it partly being created, he thought oil painting was a piece of cake!

He had little talent yet I was very surprised when he started selling what he produced.

This made me think that maybe I should try my hand at oil painting with a modicum of success. The dog club became quite a useful market with captive customers! Most dog owners like pictures of their dogs and for those interested, and willing to pay, I would photograph the dog from several angles and then construct an oil painted portrait of it, and sell it at a give-away price, really just covering the cost of materials!

I also used to enjoy building models. At school it was usually aircraft and we had extremely large playing fields where we could fly the finished product. I have built my fair share of plastic model kits and got involved in racing, and custom building $1/32^{nd}$ scale model cars, on commercial slot tracks. The cars I built were good too and usually winners. This activity virtually died when I became a dog owner.

Almost a One-Man Show

After a couple of years Terry was persuaded into taking a salesman's' job by a colleague from the past. He became the agent to sell a manufactured bracketing system that we had started using and was a real time saver. Steve had no interest in being a Foreman/Charge Hand, so I ended up with the job.

Even so, after more than five years Steve said it was the longest he had ever worked for anyone, and it was time to move on. Now I was the only skilled individual in the branch. With the hospital contract completed I could now be employed on other contracts.

As the only skilled person in the branch, I felt that I could do with some help particularly with the welding. We put an ad in the local newspaper, and only one applicant turned up. A coloured guy called Mike presented himself with a fistful of papers, presumably references, and I told him to put them away as I intended to test him.

I set up two tests, one for me, and an identical one for him, and explained to him that I would do the test first and I expected him to do his test at least as good as me since I was not a qualified welder. It was quite a simple test, but his efforts left a great deal to be desired! I needed help and as the only applicant I had to employ him, but initially I would not allow him anywhere near a welding machine! Over the next ten months since he knew the basics, I taught him to weld to my satisfaction.

Now that the hospital contract was finished, I think that Val thought I would be transferred back to Port Elizabeth, but I was the only skilled (white) man in the branch, so it was unlikely. I even tried to get her to agree to us buying a house in East London, but she was still under the impression we were only there temporarily and would not hear of it.

Eric landed a big government contract to instal two ten tonne boilers, and a new steam main at Fort Fredrick, East London's gaol. A boilers tonnage refers to its output in tonnes of steam per hour, whereas its deadweight is considerably more and installation requires the use of heavy equipment. This kept me busy for months especially as we had to run the steam main over the roof of the prison.

I noticed that the prison kennels and exercise area were right next door to the new boiler house, and I approached the Dog-Master to ask if I could be allowed to watch a training session. He agreed, and I pushed my luck a bit, and asked if other instructors from the club could come too.

There were three of us who turned up, and we ended up watching one dog-handler put his German Shepherd dog through its paces. When we asked where the rest of the dogs were, we were told they could not have more than one dog out at a time, otherwise there would be a dogfight! We concluded that our training process was far superior to theirs (we used The British Police Training & Care manual) since we had approximately one hundred dogs of varying breed and size, every Sunday morning, and I never experienced a dogfight there in 15 years!

On this contract I found that government drawings could not be a true reflection of what was required! I installed the two coal screw conveyors exactly at the angle displayed in the drawing and waited for the inspection.

The government engineer refused to accept the screw conveyors with the comment that they wouldn't work, due to the angle at which they had been installed, but I argued that they were as displayed, and we should have coal delivered to try them out. Once again, I was told straight that the conveyors wouldn't work, and I had to dismantle the installation, and do it again at a different angle! There is a clause in every government contract that states that it must be a working installation, irrespective of the specifications!

Due to the unlimited source of labour, using prisoner inmates, the working boiler house looked immaculate with painted floor, with painted, marked lanes in different colours, and not a sign of coal dust. Stuart Goddard used to use it as a sales example for John Thompson Africa (JTA), and oil to coal conversion, by taking wavering, prospective, buyers to see a working coal boiler house. Johnson & Johnson were very reluctant to buy a coal boiler for fear of coal dust ingress into their product during manufacture. Stuart must have convinced them as I commissioned their new boiler later, after joining JTA.

Chapter 10

A change of direction

Visitors

I do not remember the exact date (maybe 1975) we received more visitors from the UK when my mother brought her two sisters, Doris and Gladys, for a holiday in South Africa, and to visit us. Val hadn't been employed since we left Port Elizabeth (about 5 years), but before their arrival she instantly got herself a job working for the Divisional Council.

I was not very happy about this because it meant Rory had to come home from junior school to an empty house. I think this was more a case of making herself unavailable on a normal working day, so that the three ladies would not be able to visit her! Doris and Gladys were keen to "see South Africa" and not spend their entire time in East London but that didn't really suit my mother who wanted to spend time with Rory and me. All three of them travelled around including Cape Town, Durban and Port Elizabeth with my mother being bad company!

There were more visitors in 1978 when my mother paid us a visit with my dad's sister Ruth. It was much the same routine really and they travelled quite extensively. Towards the end my mother developed a heart problem and was hospitalised which meant they were unable to make their flight back to the UK on time. Thankfully they had taken out insurance against such things, I financed their return trip with the promise that I would be reimbursed but it did not work out smoothly due to my mother's dementia, which also led Aunt Ruth a real dance to recover her money back in the UK.

One of Terry's big complaints was that our transport wasn't really up to the job. Our main vehicle was a double cabin Volkswagen, but it only had a 1500cc engine and even with a light load, it struggled while driving against the wind! At one time I was pulled over by the Provincial Traffic Police for being overloaded as there were six of us in the cabin, and on the load area there was an oxyacetylene welding/cutting set, a petrol driven welding machine, and my toolbox.

We were escorted to a company that possessed a weighbridge, and when the vehicle was loaded on to it, I ordered everyone out, and the police made them all get back in! I was given a warning for the overload but allowed to continue as there was no alternative transport anyway. We struggled with that vehicle for five years but after Terry had left, it was replaced with an American Ford F250.

Motor Accident

A few years later we had to do some work on a Tea plantation near Lusikisiki in the Transkei which meant being accommodated on site, as there was no alternative available in the area. A short distance past Umtata the tarred roads disappear, so from that point it is all dirt roads, and it was raining too.

Just before Port St Johns I approached a blind bend and met a local bus on the wrong side of the road, and a collision was inevitable. I think the roof rack we had constructed to carry piping and ladders etc., was partially responsible for saving our lives that day. The corner of it hit the rear of the bus driver's door, and the rear near side was driven into the bank, and the momentum levered the bus back on to the correct side of the road as the Ford swung around.

The F250 was no match for the bus and was a total write-off. The steering column came down across my left leg, the windscreen was deposited like a giant jelly across my arms, the driver's door jammed shut. There was no way I could get out, and I was afraid of fire but thankfully, it did not happen mainly because the battery was completely demolished. I got my staff to use some of our piping to lever the steering column off my leg that allowed me to get free before the shock took over. The bus driver took off into the Bush, and we never saw him again! One black woman passenger in the bus was quite badly injured but a mission hospital was quite nearby, and a motorist took her there.

… police sergeant in plain clothes arrived who was quite obviously drunk, to take details of the accident, and then left without really doing anything at all!

The main road between Port St Johns, Lusikisiki and Umtata was totally blocked by the two vehicles. No mobile phones in those days, and a big queue of motorists built up in both directions, but we had to wait for the police to arrive. I got my staff, none of whom were seriously injured, to sit in the bus out of the rain, and I leaned against the bus radiator to keep warm.

One of the blocked motorists asked me what had happened to the driver of the pickup, and I replied that he was talking to him. He could not believe I had got out of the wreck alive. A police sergeant in plain clothes arrived who was quite obviously drunk, to take details of the accident, and then left without really doing anything at all!

The accident took place at 15:00, and a breakdown crew from the bus company in Umtata arrived at 19:00 to clear the road. One of the motorists offered me a lift to Umtata, but did not include my staff, so I refused to leave them, once the road was clear. Eventually the breakdown crew offered us and our kit, a lift on their pickup back to Umtata, and made all their black staff remove their wet weather clothes, and give them to my staff as it was still raining.

It was very late getting back to Umtata and the bus crew took us to three different hotels before we found one that would accommodate us! No Credit cards then and I used every cent I had to get everyone a room, and that was all. By now it was midnight, and I asked the reception if there was any chance of some food and drink, since we had not had anything all day, but the bus crew heard the refusal and said they would take me to their depot to bring something back for everyone. When they brought me back with the sustenance all my crew had already gone to bed!

I reported the accident the next morning to the Port Elizabeth office and a replacement vehicle was sent to collect us, but the driver took all day to arrive, and then expected accommodation at the hotel! There was no way (or cash) we were going to spend another night in Umtata, so he had to drive us to the bus depot to collect our gear. On that short drive I thought it was doubtful that this chap had a license, and I refused to let him drive us any further.

My left arm was now very painful, and I could not handle the column gear shift, but one of my staff sat next to me on the bench seat, and made the gear changes when I told him, (there weren't many with a 4100cc engine powering the pickup) and I worked the clutch pedal and steering wheel. I found out the next day from my doc that my wrist was broken. As the only person with a driving license, I still had to drive even with my arm in plaster!

I was later subpoenaed to appear in court at Port St Johns, but after waiting there all day they could not find whoever had issued it, and I didn't hear anything further about it! Just a wasted trip of about 150 miles and back!

Actually, Terry's job as a salesman didn't last that long, and he joined a different engineering firm that specialised in sheet metal work. For quite some time Terry had tried to convince me to join him in a venture to sell new and maintain/repair lawnmowers. He was a keen motorcyclist, and considered that as lawnmowers were powered by small two-stroke engines we could do well as a business, but I could not see a future in it. I didn't doubt our ability to do it but couldn't see that we would get enough custom.

How wrong I was! Terry started up on his own and formed a business named Mowers, which ended up as the top lawnmower business in the area over a number of years, and still is today.

Our site office at the hospital was used as our East London base, but now that the contract was complete, we had to find new premises, and we moved to a permanent building closer to the centre of town. As a family we changed addresses too over a period of several years.

After a change from one place to another, I received a phone call from my aunt Doris that my mother was in a hospital in Hereford, and if I wished to see her again then I should make tracks back to the UK as soon as possible. There was a delay of about four weeks, due to the phone being moved to a new residence, which meant I received the call quite late, so a visit to the UK was now urgent, and I was booked on a flight two days later.

UK visit 1979

It was 1979, my uncle Bert collected me from Heathrow, and delivered me to Hereford where my aunt Gladys shared her home with me, which made it very convenient to visit my mother in hospital. I visited her every day, but I don't think she even knew who I was, or that I had been away for sixteen years. My mother died after a week, and I suggested to Gladys that I would like to go and live in my mother's flat at The Lea, which used to be my home.

She didn't think I should be left on my own, even though that is what I wanted, and insisted on staying there with me! She very kindly loaned me her car for the duration of my stay. I stayed in the flat for a further two weeks, and my mother was cremated in Hereford crematorium, with memorial services in the churches of villages, Weston-Under-Penyard and The Lea.

I had hoped to be able to perhaps meet old friends during my short stay, but that wasn't possible so I wrote to a few explaining that I would be at Heathrow airport all day on the day I left, if they cared to visit me. As it happened, I was told the flight was overbooked, and even though I had a valid ticket, there was no guarantee that I would get a seat!

While I was waiting in the queue, Pat Davies arrived with her two children, to keep me company. Pat was an ex-teacher of the BGSD (British German Shepard Dog) Club in East London who now lived in the UK, and she came with a message from her husband, "If he doesn't get a seat on the plane, bring him home", for which I was eternally grateful as I did not get a seat. I did not wish to, nor have the means to return to The Lea. I asked the airline, "What happens now", as my ticket expired that day, and I was told to come back tomorrow to try again! This was not practical, and I asked for a day when I could have a guaranteed seat, and was told it would be in twelve days' time!

I stayed with Pat & Jamie for the remainder of the time except for the last weekend. After a few days I told them I should move on, but they would not hear of it and said I had to help them move house on the following weekend!

While I was in the flat at The Lea I received a letter of condolence from Fay, who had been told of my mother's passing by a family member, and she invited me to visit her family, if I could find the time. It was only a short train journey from my present place in Oxted to the Lewis family home in Billericay, and with a phone-call, a visit was arranged for Sunday lunch. So it was that Fay and I re-met after twenty-two years, and all the attractive feelings I had for her returned, but now she was a married lady and I a married man, each of us married to someone else.

The last night in the UK I was invited to stay with my uncle Percy, and after travelling to his home in Fulham I was entertained with a trip to visit Ron and Margaret and family in Orpington that same evening. I had only briefly seen Ron once since his visit to Ryeford during the War and never met Margaret, Evelyn and Jane. The next day I was treated to lunch in an English pub and later, driven to Heathrow for my flight back to South Africa.

Return to South Africa

I found that Mike, the coloured man who had been left in charge of the workshop while I was away had resigned almost as soon as I left for the UK! Little had been done during the few weeks I was away, and I still had two contracts to do, one of which was at a hospital in Umtata, 120 miles away. This was quite large, and a major part involved installing steam piping on raised supports over open ground.

I received privileged information from Eric Rix, that Bestobell had been subjected to a takeover bid on The London Stock Exchange and were closing all their subsidiaries in an effort to fend it off, which meant Albert Vaux & Co (Pty) Ltd would be closing down. I had written to Bestobell in the UK to find out the prospects of work, and I think I was told in an effort to get me to stay where I was, whereas the rest of the staff in Port Elizabeth were handed their end of year pay and told not to come back!!! Eric also tried to convince me to become self-employed and continue working with him providing the jobs and paying my salary, but I was not impressed with the idea.

The final contract was to instal a new motor to a large water pump (24 inch bore) for the East London Municipality. The connection was through a flexible coupling with a tolerance of 40 microns, but it was a huge motor that weighed 5 tonnes, and all movements had to be carried out using an overhead crane in the pumphouse. This installation took quite some considerable time.

Finally, a demonstration was arranged for approximately twenty dignitaries to attend the first running of the pump, and I and one of my black assistants, worked the whole night through to make sure everything was 100%. Just before the demo, the City Engineer asked me what I had set the tolerance for the coupling, and I told him it was between 1and 2 microns in both horizontal and vertical directions (1000 microns to 1 millimetre). "That isn't good enough." he said!!!

After the all-night session I told him that he was welcome to have the use of my toolbox if he could do any better, especially as there was a tolerance of 40 microns available. It was no trouble for him, and in front of all the dignitaries, and in his suit he set about improving my settings, and after 15 minutes the coupling was misaligned by 36 microns in one direction. "We'll test it anyway", he said, and I stood with everyone else and watched the motor destroy the coupling in minutes because he had moved the motor! It was 2 days before Christmas, and I was offered double my salary to work through the holiday period to rescue the disaster, but I refused, and it was my last job for Albert Vaux & Co.

Fay and I had become prolific letter writers again, and my brief visit to the UK had whet my appetite and I set about returning. *I must stress at this point that I had no intention of separating from my wife.* I had lived in South Africa for 16 years, and I didn't consider it unreasonable to talk about going back, compared to Val's 4 years she had spent in the UK. However, word had got around that I was going to be unemployed.

Stuart Goddard was the local agent for John Thompson Africa, and came knocking on my door, but I told him of my intention to go back to the UK. Stuart was a Yorkshireman and thought I was nuts and had set up an interview for me with his boss, the Technical Director from Cape Town. We had done a lot of boiler installations for that company, and I serviced a great deal of their boilers and burners for customers in the area.

I also had a very good understanding with the local Government Inspector, who allowed me to carry out annual boiler inspections and write the report, a requirement by law, without his attendance. A few days later after the interview I was offered the post of Commissioning Engineer in the Eastern Cape for JTA on a salary more than double what I had been previously paid, with Stuart as their area salesman. I accepted.

John Thompson Africa

Due to the Arabs holding the world to ransom with oil, JTA had sold a lot of coal-fired boilers, and indeed, I had carried out several Oil to Coal conversions on local boilers in my previous job, but I knew little about coal burning. I had to go to the parent company in Cape Town for a period of one month to familiarise myself with the product I had to service.

The daunting part for me was when I was placed in the Panel Shop. I knew somewhat more than basic electrics, but I was given an empty panel, an electrical drawing, and all the necessary kit to make up a working panel that would be attached to a boiler and sold! It took me a couple of days whereas the normal staff took less than a day, but eventually when it was tested, one connection needed adjustment, so I was quite relieved. This would not be required of me again but gave me an insight of the numbered terminals and what was their purpose during operation – an aid to troubleshooting. Although I did not make the electrical power connection on site, as the Commissioning Engineer I had to make all the others after a boiler was delivered to a customer as several parts were delivered separately.

Stuart felt that he needed help, so my familiarisation was cut short to three weeks, and I was given my company car to drive back to East London from Cape Town. Before I did any commissioning, I had to understudy one of the experienced engineers to make sure I worked to the JTA standard. I cannot remember his name now but later he became head of the commissioning section of JTA, so I could not have had better instruction.

Stuart was selling boilers almost daily and I was spending up to three weeks per month in Port Elizabeth or the surrounding district commissioning them! Generally, it would take a working week to complete one, depending on size, but bigger ones would take a lot longer and they would vary from 2 ½ tonnes of steam per hour for small boilers, to 23 tonnes per hour for a top of the range. I also had to spend a month in Johannesburg assisting the engineers who were swamped by the number of sales.

I remember one of these giants that was installed in the Koo Canning factory in East London. It was more than a boiler installation in that the new boiler house pipework had to be connected to the factory existing steam main and the customer wanted a performance test before it was handed over. It took several weeks to install, and it was to be my first ever Load test. A large group of technical people were flown in from Cape Town and it was successfully carried out over several hours and the twenty odd tonnes of steam produced per hour were exhausted to atmosphere through a ten-inch main, which upset all the neighbours due to the noise.

It was all carried out at the normal operating pressure of a JTA boiler (150 psi), but the company wanted to use it at a lower pressure and once the boiler was accepted, I had to set it up at the lower working pressure (100 psi). The pipework was connected to the steam main through a brand-new 10 inch valve supplied by the customer, and I fired the boiler, giving instruction to the resident boiler watchmen at the same time.

... the new isolating valve had broken as soon as the boilerman opened it and scalded him to death!!!

The safety valves were set to lift at the lower operating pressure, the main stop valve was opened, and I instructed one of the boilermen that he could connect up to the main by opening the isolating valve in the old boiler house once they were ready. Off he went and moments later I heard a pop which I thought was the safety valves opening and went outside to look. What I saw was steam pouring freely out of the old boiler house in all directions. I ran back into the new boiler house to close the main stop valve of the new boiler. The bottom of the new isolating valve had broken as soon as the boilerman opened it and scalded him to death!!! I had to attend the subsequent inquiry, and it was found that the Chinese manufactured steam valve was of substandard quality and had failed.

LETTING OFF STEAM

I had to commission a new boiler at the South African Railway yard in Uitenhage and I turned up one morning to find a seven-ton truck parked where I normally parked my car. I parked behind the truck and then realised I could not see its driving mirrors and I did not want the truck being reversed into my car because the driver could not see it! I reversed back down the road for at least fifty metres, parked the car and walked to the boiler house.

While I was changing into my overalls, a boilerman came in and said, "That truck has reversed into your car"! Later that day I managed to drive to my hotel in Port Elizabeth with a damaged radiator, but the car was obviously not going to get me back to East London. I reported it to my office and told them I would hire a car to drive back and leave the car for repair at a garage, but Stuart told me to get on a plane to fly back.

1980 and I received a letter from Fay telling me that she had separated from her husband and she and her two daughters had left the family home and they were staying with friends. She also told me that she would like to visit South Africa. After some months of planning, both sides of the equator, I took two weeks holiday, told Val I had more work in Johannesburg and flew there to meet Fay when she arrived for three weeks holiday.

After a couple of days, we flew back to East London to collect my car and drove to Port Alfred until I had to return to work. I had boilers to commission but that meant I had to be accommodated in hotels anyway, until Fay's holiday was complete, and she went back to the UK for Christmas. I felt no guilt whatsoever after all the years of absolute fidelity, even though the previous three weeks had been underhand, but I guess my patience had worn very thin by then!

Chapter 11

Second visit to the UK

Seeking work

I was now very keen to return to the UK and tested JTA management to see if it was possible to get some study leave. I did not wish to 'burn my bridges' by resigning and find I could not find work there and have to come back. I had broached the subject with Val and there had been an element of agreement that I would try a sample visit of six months alone working in the UK maybe with the help of JTA or even Bestobell, but I was offered three months instead of the six months I would have liked and had to resign anyway.

If I found a good position in the UK, the plan would be to return to South Africa to wind up my position in South Africa and then we would return to work. I gave the entire contents of my bank account to Val so that she could have finance while I was away and took a flight to the UK and arrived on 1st April 1981, where Fay met me and drove me to her new home in Wickford. It was so different being in an area where nobody knew me after leaving an environment where I was well known and had a very good reputation both socially and in the engineering world.

I guess it was a bad time to be seeking work in the UK. I contacted John Thompson UK and had an interview in the London offices but there were no vacancies. I wrote to companies looking for staff enclosing copies of my experience and generally got no reply! A company that specialised in coal handling equipment were very interested and I drove up to Newcastle for an interview and the result sounded quite promising when I was told I had a job, and they would write to me when to start. That letter is either still coming or was lost in the post! Generally, it was a lost cause, and I knew I had to return to South Africa where there was no problem of unemployment.

Nearing the 6 month deadline, I received an invitation to an interview for the job of manager of a section of west London for Associated Heating Services (AHS). It didn't really suit as we were living in Essex, but decisions could be made if the job was available. I felt sorry for Julie who came just for the ride and had to wait for two hours in the car while I was interviewed and I was offered the job, as long as I had a UK driving license.

As I no longer had one I thanked them and said there was little chance of my getting one considering how long one had to wait for a test, but I was advised to go to a driving school and explain that a job was on the line, and they would get me an early test. I signed for a course with British School of Motoring and had hardly started it when I was told I had a test allocated. I took the test, passed it and advised AHS and was told they had decided to promote within the company, and I would not be employed after all. All that was left was for me to keep my word to return to South Africa after almost 8 months in the UK.

John Thompson Africa again

It was a heart-rending decision to go back, and I didn't really know what I was going to do as I had resigned a good job from JTA when I left. That was when I received the second big shock in my life. Later that day when I got back home Val told me, *"When I watched you get on that plane to fly to the UK I didn't think I would ever see you again"!* This, after 23 years of marriage, she thought I would do that, abandon her and my son, and also, after the agreement that we all would return to the UK if I were successful in landing a good job there. I could see now that she had no intention of joining me in the UK whatever happened. I must admit that it was highly unlikely now after all the time Fay and I had spent together and there was little point in continuing with my sham marriage.

The following morning, I phoned Stuart to see if there was any chance of work with JTA again. I was told there was no chance in East London but possibilities in Johannesburg and Durban but I would need to visit the office later so we could talk about it. Val's only interest in moving house would be to go back to Port Elizabeth, where her mother and sister lived, so Johannesburg or Durban were out of the question, and the immediate break up of our marriage was unlikely.

I don't know if Stuart did some string pulling but by the time there was any discussion, I was offered my old job back, but I had to share my office with the guy who replaced me while I was away (I've forgotten his name, but it could be Allan). My new colleague was electrically qualified rather than with a mechanical bias, but we worked separately anyway. It did not take long to get back into my old routine. Stuart was eventually transferred to the Johannesburg office and replaced by Keith Hodgett in East London.

Having left the UK in November, Fay and I continued to correspond with the intention of finding a way to live together now that she had obtained a divorce. She eventually solved the problem when I was told she had sold her house and was coming to South Africa with her two daughters right away in September 1982! I told Val I was leaving and made a clean breast of my recent behaviour.

East London is a holiday destination for some South Africans, and I managed to organise some temporary accommodation for all of us for a short while. I met Fay, Jacky and Julie in Johannesburg and we spent a few days there. A visit to Stuart in the JTA office and I was loaned a car so that we could move about.

Bullitt, CD Ex, UD Ex, WD

That was his full title after his career and apart from leaving Val, I had also left Bullitt! I still maintained my teaching class at the dog club, and I would collect him on Sunday mornings and for any functions. There eventually came a time when I received a call from Val telling me she could not get Bullitt to come out of his kennel, so I went to see what the problem was. He exited the kennel as soon as he heard my voice, but he was obviously very sick, and we had to take him to the veterinary surgery. The diagnosis was not good, that his essential organs had failed, and he would have to be put down. He was 11 years old.

To my surprise Val was extremely upset, and although I loved him dearly, to soften the blow I told her that it was just a dog, and there could always be a replacement, even though I felt a great sorrow at the loss of my old friend. I was then subjected to a tirade from Val about how I had no feelings for the old dog, and that hurt very deeply, and this from someone who never wanted him in the house! I had no dog now but maintained my interest in the dog club, and continued teaching and made myself available as a judge for local and Championship shows.

The Arab restriction on oil faded away but we were still selling coal-fired boilers although not quite so prolifically, so I spent some of my time doing maintenance in between commissioning. Keith Hodgett was an ex-Hamworthy employee at some time and familiarised me with the Hamworthy Rotary Cup oil burner. There were JTA customers who owned boilers that were fired in this way, and they were getting very poor service from Hamworthy and Keith persuaded them to allow us to service their burners.

Soon afterwards, I was summoned into Keith's office to discuss the reason for my request to be transferred to the Johannesburg office which was a real surprise to me as I had done no such thing. It appeared that Stuart had set this up and had lied about the request. I was a stranger to the Transvaal area as well, so I would hardly want to leave an area where I was so very well known.

At about this time Jacky decided she did not want to live in South Africa and after trying to persuade her to stay, we set about planning for her to return to the UK. Fay, Jacky and Julie were in the country on holiday so there was no restriction requiring her to stay and she had been here for six weeks.

John Thompson Africa had a policy of, "Is it fair to the customer and to JTA?" And similarly, "Is it fair to JTA and to the employee?". I had a boiler to commission in a place near the border of Lesotho and South Africa, and I returned to the East London office late on a Friday afternoon when I was told there had been a breakdown in a big factory in Port Elizabeth that needed fixing immediately.

I said I would leave at 04:00 on Saturday morning and Alan agreed to come with me, but independently. A three-hour drive and I was on site at 07:00 and neither of the coal-fired boilers were working. I cannot remember the fault, but we worked all day and both boilers were operating on line by 18:00 and we left to go to the hotel. After dinner we drove back across Port Elizabeth to confirm that the boilers were still working. We spent Sunday on site making sure it was all working properly and drove back to East London later in the afternoon.

Tuesday was Republic Day 1983 and a holiday, but we were all given the Monday as a holiday too as part of our allocation. I told Allan that I would come into the office to write the report, which had to be sent to Head Office by the end of the month (Tuesday), and to stay at home with his young family.

Resignation

We were allowed to take a day off in lieu of a free day that we worked as compensation for overtime, but we were not allowed to take more than one day at a time. For instance, Friday and Monday were deemed consecutive and both could not be taken at once. I thought this was unfair since I had just worked three consecutive free days, lost a weekend, but I could only take one day at a time as compensation, so I wrote my letter of resignation.

It was a decision I had thought about all the time I was enjoying my one free day, and I had no idea what I was going to do afterwards! I had to give a full months' notice so there was time to think about it.

Chapter 12
Self-Employment

Steam expert

We decided that as I was so well known in the area, and had become known as a steam expert, that I should be able to carry on much the same as I had been doing, without the boiler commissioning. I bought a new Mazda pickup as my transport, and the intention was to advise local boiler operators during the first week, that I had left JTA, and was working for my own account. A little incident unintentionally stole that time away from me though!

> *Julie borrowed the Datsun on a Saturday evening. The next thing we knew a male and female police officer were standing on the doorstep on Sunday morning advising that she was in a police cell...*

Whereas the pickup was the only transport we had I did not think it was good enough for use socially and we bought a second-hand Datsun 1200 Sport from a dog club member that I was aware of its history, to fill this situation. Julie needed a car for a social evening, and she borrowed the Datsun on a Saturday evening. The next thing we knew a male and female police officer were standing on the doorstep on Sunday morning advising that she was in a police cell and would need bail to get out!

Once the bail was paid Julie related her side of the story. She had been arrested for driving whilst under the influence of alcohol and locked up. As it was a weekend, we were not allowed to get the car back from the pound until Monday, when I asked about recovering the little Datsun. I was told there was some slight scratching on the passenger side, and some damage to the stationery car she had hit!

The next morning, I drove to the premises of the owner of the car to view the damage. I found that it was easily possible to access the interior of the boot of a Chevrolet Chevvy Two quite comfortably without lifting the boot lid. I did not consider this to be light scratching and wondered what the vehicle that had caused this looked like!! The Chevvy had also been adapted for the use of a disabled person and I agreed to get it repaired myself.

I had rented workshop premises from 'Chalky' Shonknecht, a good friend who ran his own machine shop, and the car was delivered there. I went to a scrapyard and bought the rear half of a Chevvy Two body of the same vintage and used half of it to replace the damaged section, but I was concerned about the cost of matching the original paint, or even a complete respray since I no longer had an income. On the Friday the disabled man's two sons arrived to assess the situation and said the car was now in a better condition than before the accident and I need not paint it at all! I was quite relieved, and they drove the car away. Now I could start my business. The repairs to the little Datsun could wait and I would rebuild it completely, since that was what was needed, when I had time. Now I could apply my time to the new business of Jeff Deacon's Boiler & Burner Services.

LETTING OFF STEAM

Boiler and Burner Services

A regular customer when I worked for Albert Vaux was a dry cleaner in King Williams Town and he was having problems with his boiler as it kept locking out. Dry cleaners use a lot of thermodynamic steam traps on their equipment that send very hot condensate back to the feed tank in the boiler house. The consequence was that water in the feed tank would boil, and the boiler feed pumps could not supply the very hot water to the boiler, so the boiler would lock out due to low water.

I suggested to the owner that I could construct a cooler where the condensate could pass through, and the heated water could be used as a hot water supply for his washing machines in the laundry, a bonus! He would have free hot water every day except Mondays, the first load of the week. I also explained that if he didn't use the hot water, he would have to throw it away or the boiler problem would return.

I bought a 100-gallon tank of cement construction and made a bracket to support it. I constructed a coil from copper tubing to sit inside it and installed it in the condensate return line, and connected the water supply to the tank, after mounting the bracket to the outside of the building, using the existing immersion heater inside as a counterbalance. I stood on top of the canopy on my pickup to do this, and then opened the water supply to the tank.

After approximately half an hour I heard a noise outside, and went to investigate, only to find the weight of water in the tank had torn it off the side of the building, but luckily, I had moved my pickup! The poor construction of the building could not support the tank with almost half a ton of water in it and the cement tank had been shattered completely. The reinstallation meant I made no profit from my first 'big' job as I had to purchase another tank, and use a more substantial mounting for it. The overall plan worked extremely well.

Julie was not sure if she wanted to continue living in South Africa or return to the UK, and she went back to live with her father for a while in an attempt to make up her mind. She was away for 11 months, and her return brought us a few surprises! Fay went to Johannesburg to meet her and I met them both at East London airport, and we were both surprised at the figure that exited the aircraft. I'm not sure whether South Africa was ready for Julie at this time!

Gilly Potter

In the last couple of weeks at JTA I saw drawings of a new government project at Ncora in the Transkei, for an asparagus factory which included a new boiler, plus the complete steam installation. I felt it was quite a recommendation for me when the Consulting Engineer of the project, 'Gilly' Potter, offered the steam installation to me, as JTA only wanted the boiler sale and installation.

I tried to explain that it was far too big a project for a one man show with just a toolbox, and no staff, to take it on, but Gilly would not accept the refusal, and told me the only reason it had been offered to JTA was because I worked there! I couldn't quite understand his thinking on this as I didn't physically do installation work at JTA. My resignation had upset more than a few plans!

It was explained to me that the client would supply all the labour and heavy tools I required, and supply the accommodation, as the site was really 'in the sticks'. Gilly had been one of the consulting engineers for the hospital contract, and was aware of my capabilities, so I realised that they were intent on using my labour, no matter what I said, and I was guaranteed payment. Really, I was just quoting for my labour and travelling expenses, which was a new experience in itself, and there was a saving for the client as I did not have JTA's overheads.

I found it amusing that I was not asked to commission the new boiler by JTA since I was already on site, but I suppose it was too soon after my resignation, and I had more than enough to do. I installed the steam main, roughly about a 100 metres, half of which was at high level over open ground with the supports provided by the client. The idea of this was that the factory would expand towards the boiler house in the future, and the steam main would end up under cover.

Now that steam was available, I was asked to quote on various connections to pieces of equipment as it arrived. A client's engineer in Cape Town considered my price for the first one was too expensive, and flew in to look at the drawing, and changed the reducing valves I intended to use. I told him, and the client, that with the alterations it wouldn't work, but I was instructed to instal it his way! I never saw him again after the initial run as the equipment never reached operating temperature after an hour, something that should have taken minutes. The plant manager was irate, and told the engineer to return to Cape Town in no uncertain terms, and I was instructed to remove the installation and redo it as I had originally planned.

The project became a very good starter for me and set me up very nicely as I was well paid. Gilly was quite useful too, and other government contracts came my way thanks to him. He used to give me inside information as to what was expected, when it came to quoting, and submitting a price, although I didn't allow it to restrict my costing.

Another one of Gilly's recommendations was for some modifications to a brewery in Mdantsane, the black township outside of East London. Once again, I tried to refuse the contract as some of the prices of equipment were quite eye-watering to me as a one-man show, but Gilly was insistent, and I ended up with the best price for the tender. It also meant a reunion with Steve, although not physical assistance, who had been appointed as the brewery's resident fitter. The job went well but I was never happy about driving into any of the townships.

Even so, I ended up commissioning three oil-fired boilers at the new Mdantsane prison. The job was straight forward enough but my black assistant didn't turn up for work for several days while I was doing the job. It was not a big drawback, but I objected to his absence with no notification or reason. When he did eventually arrive for work, he explained that he had been a resident of the prison where I was working!

Smoke

I was invited to investigate a problem with a Bencor boiler in Port Elizabeth that was producing a lot of black smoke, and the company had been threatened with closure if it was not remedied. I was also unaware that a great deal of combustion companies throughout the country, had already tried to remedy the problem without success.

The burner was using Heavy Fuel Oil (HFO) which is very thick and requires heating to even move it at all. The factory continued to operate while I was there, and the boiler could not be permanently shut down for me to do a thorough job, so the work was really intermittent. These circumstances made the work very difficult, and I had to concede that I could not solve the problem and returned to East London.

A couple of years later the same problem occurred in East London when a tyre retreading company were threatened with closure due to complaints from The Mercedes Motor company, that soot from their boiler was being deposited onto parked brand new motor cars. This time I told the owner of the tyre company that I was prepared to investigate, but I could not guarantee that I could solve the problem, however, I still wished to be paid for the time I spent on their premises, and he agreed.

The circumstances were much the same, but the intermittent times were a little longer. I discovered that from time to time the fuel oil heater would be stripped for cleaning, and due to poor construction, the heater could be reassembled differently. This meant that the thermostat controlling temperature of the oil being fed to the burner could end up in the wrong place in the heater, and the oil would arrive at the burner at constantly varying temperatures.

> *... received news that Jacky was getting married, and of course Fay had to return to the UK to be the mother of the bride.*

I modified the equipment to prevent the variable assembly to maintain the position of the thermostat and presented my bill to the plant manager. I also told him I could not improve the present condition of smoke leaving the chimney stack and he instructed his staff to light up the boiler!!! He could not believe that the boiler was actually working at the time since the stack was smoke free! This time I did get paid. I would have loved to go to Port Elizabeth for a second attempt, but the company had replaced their oil-fired boiler and bought a coal-fired unit.

We received news that Jacky was getting married, and of course Fay had to return to the UK to be the Mother of the Bride.

JTA did eventually ask me to commission boilers for them, presumably because they no longer had a local engineer and would have to fly one in. I was asked to recommission a new installation of an oil to coal conversion at Berkshire International. It was an original JTA boiler, but the burner had been removed and replaced with a chain-grate stoker.

While it was warming through quite a large crowd of the customer's employees came into the boiler house to watch what was happening. As the pressure in the boiler increased the safety valves began to discharge steam and I had to reset them. I had to reset them several times which I found to be quite strange, until I noticed that the level of water in the boiler was dropping, despite the feed pump running continuously!

With the water level reducing, I dumped the fire from the stoker and started to shut the boiler down when one of the local fitters climbed up the front of the boiler, and accidentally bumped the steam pressure gauge on the boiler. I suddenly found myself all alone in the boiler house when the needle on the pressure gauge swung round the dial to more than double the working pressure of the boiler! I spent some considerable time, quite scared, backing off the safety valves to reduce the pressure in the boiler. The valves and fittings fitted to the boiler were not structurally safe to work at that pressure, and any one of them could have failed at any time, including the safety valves! I reported the incident to the Government inspector and spent some time with him inside the boiler when he inspected it several days later. There was no distortion or damage to the boiler tube plates and I was allowed to successfully complete the job a few days later.

Another dog

With Julie's birthday approaching Fay and I were reminded by Julie that she would like a dog of her own. By shopping around the clubs I knew in the Eastern Cape, we found a breeder in Port Elizabeth that had a litter of Golden Retrievers to sell. We all travelled to Port Elizabeth to view the litter and returned with a puppy as Julie's birthday present that was eventually named Tuppence, and she responded very well to training.

After she was almost a mature adult, I was conned one Sunday at the dog club by a Doberman breeder (Sheila Meyer) who placed a puppy in my arms, and told me it was a gift! He became known as Titan but was of a different character to Bullitt. I do not think Sheila had any ulterior motive, but being a good quality Doberman, he would not have progressed in the breed ring as he had a misshapen left ear. I was not interested in the breed ring at all so that was immaterial.

LETTING OFF STEAM

There were times when I needed the help of a skilled tradesman and while working on the contract at Ncora I met Macolm who was a wheelwright who made himself available if extra labour was required. He lived in Cathcart and if he was assisting me on a contract, he would lodge with us in East London.

It must have been quite a lucrative situation for him as I never made any money while he was helping me! One particular instance was when I had to remove seven redundant boilers from a government property in Queenstown and Malcolm in Cathcart was quite close instead of 120 miles away from me. I hired a 15-tonne crane that had to travel there from East London and left Malcolm to do the job. At the end of the day I was informed that the crane was incapable of doing the lifts and had returned to East London. South African Railways had a 40-tonne crane in Queenstown on a temporary assignment and allowed me to hire it for one day but at considerable cost. Later that day Malcolm told me that the white crane driver said he couldn't do the lift because the reach was too far!

I have had to pay for the hire of two cranes and the job still had to be done, so I decided I had to do it myself. I hired the 15-tonne crane again and went to site where we removed five of the seven boilers with comparative ease. The reach for the last two boilers was at the cranes limit and obviously very difficult, and I told the black crane driver that he would have to leave them there and I would have to find another method of removal. His reply to me was, "Boss, I did not drive all this way to not do the job!". The Health and Safety Rules were stretched quite extensively, but the last two boilers were removed. I have no idea why there was so much difficulty with the previous efforts and I just had to accept the loss. Malcolm used to make sure he always scored and although he had helped me several times, it was his last employment with me.

Tendering

There was a period when engineering jobs were scarce, and tenders were hard to come by. I found myself competing with air conditioning companies for steam and boiler work.

A big government tender was offered involving separate tenders for four wide-spread country mission hospitals boiler houses that even Gilly realised was far too big for me in total. All of them was for work in the boiler house and I decided to tender for the one main boiler house. It was supply and instal materials that were supplied by Bestobell and the local representative, whom I knew very well, assured me that I had the best price for their products. My complete tender was just under 60,000 Rand, and I was stunned to find that a big air-conditioning company had beaten me into second place!

Their price had totally wiped out all my labour costs, in excess of 15000 Rand, and meant they were doing the job for nothing! On the strength of this I tendered on one of the smaller hospitals and exactly the same thing happened, so I did not bother with the other two hospitals.

Sometime later I was asked to commission a second-hand coal-fired boiler for a new textile company in the Transkei. They were not best pleased when I said I could not do the job without some coal and without consulting me, they ordered 50 tonnes of the wrong size coal! Considering they did not intend going into production immediately, they could have borrowed sufficient coal from one of the other factories in the area.

While I was there, I heard that they needed a complete steam installation which involved multiple various sized reducing valves, so I approached the new Bestobell representative for the supply. He said he would relieve me of the cost if I gave him a price for my labour, and between us we designed the complete installation, and the tender was submitted in his company's name. Since the local staff did not know I was involved, I was told various stories about the 'ludicrously' expensive tenders they had received for the complete steam installation.

They eventually made a saving by doing the installation themselves, knocking more than 50000 Rand off our quotation, by doing the job for 7000 Rand. Needless to say, it didn't work with the wrong valves and piping used, and the dyeing machines and driers never came close to reaching their operating temperatures. I never did find out how they progressed.

Return to the UK

Once again, I found training a Doberman pup to be hard work, probably because a lot of my training time was to teaching other people and Titan didn't get the service that he needed.

One Sunday morning I was chatting with a group of handlers after training, with the dogs running free in the park, and I called Titan to come back as it was time to go home. I was so pleased because he responded instantly for the first time in his life, and I prepared to give him the praise and welcome he deserved. As he reached the group, a GSD sitting with us on lead, nipped Titan just behind his right leg, and due to his speed, he was ripped open the full length of his body like a zip fastener!

I had to leave him with the Vet, who opened on a Sunday just for me, where he received twenty-one stitches. It was unfortunate as a couple were coming to see him that afternoon with a view to keeping him, as Fay and I had decided to return to the UK, and we could not take him with us. It did a lot of harm to Titan mentally as he would attack any GSD on sight from that day forward! He was 18 months old.

Despite the fact that we were doing so well, Fay and I decided that South Africa was not going to care for us in our latter years in the way that the United Kingdom does. We thought that the longer we left it then the chances of employment in the UK were reduced and now, in 1988 I was already fifty-two.

Chapter 13

Permanent return to the UK

Unemployed again

Jacky met us at Heathrow airport in 1998, and we were driven to Ipswich by one of her neighbours, but we had still not chosen where we would finally live. In the meantime, we lodged with David and Jacky until we could find some employment. Fay signed up with an employment agency that offered temporary employment and was soon working again.

> ...*I got underneath the Vauxhall Chevette and started removing the gearbox.*

Jacky had a car which she didn't use, mainly because it had a problem with the gearbox and was parked outside the house. A pre-lunch drink was suggested on the Sunday, and we all trooped down to the local pub with the next-door neighbour. I don't know if David and the neighbour doubted my capabilities, but it was considered a joke when I suggested that the car could be fixed without taking it to a garage, if I was allowed to look at it.

Once we had returned, and despite some slight rain, and using David's limited toolkit, I got underneath the Vauxhall Chevette and started removing the gearbox. Realising my difficulty, Fay went out and bought a set of socket spanners which made the job a lot easier. Once the gearbox and clutch were removed, I found that the small bush that accommodated the main spindle from the gearbox in the flywheel of the engine had become dislodged and was jammed between the main and slave clutch plates, preventing selection for engagement. I replaced the bush and secured it with superglue(!), and then replaced the clutch and gearbox. The car was now serviceable again although I had destroyed the clothes I had been wearing while doing the job!

Jacky used to get a coach to work every day, so the car wasn't used at all. As Fay needed to get to various places to work, I used Jacky's car to deliver her to work. There was still a fault with the car and Jacky refused to drive it! It used to run well but if it had to stop, such as for traffic lights, it would stall as soon as it was necessary to drive on and was reluctant to restart! It was quite embarrassing to be at the front of a queue of cars being unable to move. I eventually traced the fault to a broken gasket at the top of the carburettor and replaced it with one I made from paper, but Jacky would still not drive it.

We were still waiting for our car that we had shipped to the UK along with furniture, tools and other effects, in a container. It was to be an estimated delivery within six weeks, but we had not received any news of it now after two months. Jacky's car became very useful when I was granted an interview for a job with Babcock Contractors in Crawley, having written letters to several companies looking for work. Fay came with me when I drove to Crawley and waited while I took the interview.

Before the interview I was asked two questions prior to the interview that required a 'Yes or No' answer. I was asked," Are you prepared to work anywhere in the World, and this includes Northern Ireland and Russia?", and "Are you prepared to work with any material, and this includes radio-active material?". It occurred to me that to answer "No" to either question would mean that there would be no interview, so I said "Yes". I had assumed that Babcock were the boiler manufacturer, but I was told this was not the case.

Babcock Contractors Ltd

I was offered a job as a Commissioning engineer, but it was somewhat different from my previous positions. I was to report to Aldermaston where nuclear warheads were being manufactured, as part of a commissioning team of a new water cleansing plant being built, and I would be accommodated at a Reading pub, "The Winning Hand".

This was engineering of a different kind to me since I did not need any tools and was not required to wear overalls. There was a very high level of security, and I was vetted for a pass for entry to the site, which had to be surrendered every evening on leaving the site. I found it difficult to maintain a great deal of interest in the job since I did not have to do any manual labour. There were approximately forty engineers of varying disciplines in the office. Initially I was given a host of manuals, drawings, and documents to read to become familiar with the site, and what we were trying to achieve. I was eventually shown around the installation which was totally constructed of stainless steel by a colleague of a similar level to my own.

Aldermaston AWE

Fay found some accommodation for us in Reading, and after we heard that our container had arrived in Kingston upon Hull, we would be required to collect the car as the

Customs official could not access the boot and wished to examine the contents.

I was asked why I had locked it, which I found rather a strange question when I was required to hand over the vehicle, and all our possessions to a bunch of strangers for a delivery over six thousand miles! A key was available for them to drive the car but would not provide access to any storage area. My toolboxes were padlocked shut and one of them had the lid tack-welded shut to prevent unauthorised entry. We caught a train to Hull and stayed the night at a hotel having booked a taxi to take us to the docks the next morning.

I had paid for a 20-foot container to accommodate our possessions, but I found that they had been put into a 40-foot container along with the effects and possessions, plus two more motor cars of two other people and it had been broken into! I was quite annoyed to find this out but was told that we were lucky in that three or four containers had been lost at sea during transit!

The boot of the car was unlocked, and I was made to take everything out of it but it was not of any interest to the Customs official and it was all put back in. He insisted that I open all my toolboxes and I opened one to get a hammer and chisel to free the others from the welds and pop rivets. Once open, the official said, "I'm not going through that lot!", and I was allowed to close them up again! Arrangements were made for the delivery of everything to be made to our home in Reading, and after a jump start for the car, we were allowed to drive back. It was good to be in a familiar vehicle again.

Quite frequently I would arrive at work only to find a long queue waiting to get in! Every vehicle had to be inspected before any passes were handed out. I found it amusing that after opening the bonnet of the car, the driver was asked if everything was normal, and nothing extra had been installed in the engine compartment. Some of the engineers a lot better qualified than me used to say they didn't know, and had no idea what it should look like, and meant it!!!

After four months working at Aldermaston, during Easter weekend I received a call from a senior engineer and was told not to come to work after the holiday as my pass had been cancelled. This was a process that implied I was a security risk although I cannot understand why it had taken so long. I wasn't sure what to do but was advised to go to Head Office in Crawley. I drove there and the management was in a quandary about where to employ me, as I had been employed specifically to work at Aldermaston, so I spent a few days driving from Reading to Crawley to really just waste time in the office!

Durocs Ltd

A place was found for me on a site near Tilbury called Linford where a new plant to produce light weight concrete was under construction. The entire plant was computer controlled and I found the work fascinating despite my ignorance of the technique.

Actually, I was not particularly enamoured at driving a desk, but I still was not allowed any involvement in the actual physical installation. Things improved though as parts of the plant were tested as the installation progressed. Fay did her usual thing and found us somewhere to live in the town of Corringham, and also, found herself a job as a temporary office assistant.

To produce the product, a chemical compound called the 'Cake' was discharged as a liquid into a mould that was 7 metres long and about 2 ½ metres wide and 1 ½ metres high. This was on a transporter called a Car, which would travel at high speed to a pre-selected conveyor and placed upon it, the mould would travel to a predetermined spot in a flash off area. In all of this movement there was to be a smooth process with no sudden stops and starts, or the contents would behave just like baking a cake in the oven, and collapse.

There was a time limit to this as several moulds had to be delivered into the flash off area, and each mould put in the correct spot on the conveyor. During this time the cake would rise inside the mould to virtually fill the entire mould over a period of about 2 hours.

After the necessary time in the flash off area, each mould would be delivered to another car, and transported to an area where the cake could be removed from the mould and be of sufficient consistency to be handled by a bespoke crane, and yet able to be cut through with piano wire! The entire processed cake would then be loaded into an autoclave to be cured over several hours.

It was about a year since we left South Africa that Rory informed me that Val was in hospital seriously ill, but I was in no position to make a visit and Rory considered it unnecessary. Late in October another call told me Val had died of cancer, and he was attending to her estate. Rory sent me a copy of her death certificate sometime later and I was surprised to see it indicated she was a widow, which implied I was deceased!

We made regular trips to Ipswich to visit Jacky and David and later to view properties. We eventually chose a house in Trafalgar Close in Ipswich which was nothing out of the ordinary, but had a very attractive garden, complete with waterfall.

I suppose I was somewhat naïve as I decided to leave my application for leave until the job at Linford was complete, but Babcock Contractors had other ideas, and sent me to a site in Scotland near Kirkaldy. I strongly objected to this as it was my intention to move into the new house at the start of my leave, and have the next two weeks to settle in. I drove to the new site on a Monday and was allowed to drive back home on the Thursday, a round trip of approximately 1000 miles, to move in during the weekend! Having arrived on site I saw nothing pressing that required my immediate presence.

Chapter 14

Scotland

Gas production from coal

British Gas were developing a plant that allowed poor quality coal to be converted into brickettes that could be used by undeveloped countries to produce gas, and we were commissioning the experimental plant. I was not particularly happy about the situation since I had just bought a house that I would only see once a fortnight, while I lived in digs in Kirkaldy, and two very long drives during a weekend that enabled me to do it. This continued for a year when I hoped a new post would be more convenient.

Ravenscraig Steelworks

My hopes were short-lived however when I found myself at Ravenscraig steelworks in Wishaw, now on the other side of Scotland, near Glasgow. In a way it was more convenient, but I was now on shiftwork while we commissioned a coke oven. We had to do four-night shifts, 23:00 to 07:00, four afternoon shifts, 15:00 to 23:00, and four-day shifts, 07:00 to 15:00, when we were free for the next 4 days. With a drive home after the afternoon shift, we would have the 4 free days, plus the time to drive back to Scotland before we took on the night shift. It was hard on the Toyota Cressida and disaster was to follow.

One evening I was driving north in the rain for my night shift when I caught up to a line of HGVs on the A66, a road that crosses the Pennines. The road is interspersed with dual and single carriageway sections, and one needs to pass very quickly when the opportunity is available, to make good progress.

Near the top I managed to pass the line, but due to the rain and the lights of oncoming vehicles being reflected off the wet road, I did not see something lying in the road. Whatever it was punctured both of the near-side tyres with instant deflation as I drove over it, tore the exhaust pipe from the engine manifold, fractured the fuel line, and tore a big hole in the passenger side floor. I was impressed with the Toyota as despite the damage, it still maintained a straight line at speed. I managed to reach the filling station at the top of the Pennines where I could use a phone to get help, and also to advise my colleague that I would probably be late for my shift. This was about 19:00, and the AA advised me that someone would be with me in an hour. After 2 hours waiting, I phoned again and was assured that someone would be with me within the hour! The filling station closed at 22:00 so I sat in the car to wait for the help and keep out of the rain. An AA van eventually arrived about 22:30, and the driver told me he had driven from Workington and had only ventured out in the storm as a woman was stuck on the top of the Pennines!

I suppose I should be grateful to the person who gave him the wrong information, but there was no-one else there but me, so he hitched up my car and set out to deliver me to Wishaw. I was taken to an AA depot about halfway to Glasgow where my car was loaded onto a trailer, and a new driver was to take me the rest of the way. We decided to drop the car off in the yard of a Tyre and Exhaust company in Wishaw that allowed the driver to return home, and I walked to the Steelworks for my night shift. This was one time that I was extremely thankful for taking out the extra insurance of a breakdown with the AA. It was 03:00!

I promised my colleague that I would make up the time he had stood in for me, and after my shift I walked back to the Tyre and Exhaust place where the car had been parked. I asked them to replace the two burst tyres and to repair the exhaust, but the manager refused to do anything with the exhaust until the fuel line had been repaired.

I was in a Catch 22 situation as I could not move the car with no exhaust and a damaged fuel supply, so I had to fix the fuel line myself. Not knowing the area at all, I spent hours walking the streets until I found the parts I needed to repair the broken fuel pipe. Once I had done it, it did not take them long to fit a new exhaust pipe, and the new tyres were already in place. It was late in the day by the time I got back to my digs for a meal and to prepare for my night shift! The work was mainly recording temperatures every hour so not stressful but more a case of staying awake as I would be alone on site. I repaired the hole in the floor while I was home after the round of shifts making the car sound again.

I was called into the manager's office and asked the question, "How would you like to go to Hong Kong?"

Having moved house Julie had problems with Tuppence as she was being attacked in their garden by monkeys! It was agreed that Tuppence would be sent to us in the UK where she would have to undergo a period of quarantine. She was housed some distance away, and after 3 months we did what I later considered to be a big mistake, we went to visit her!

Of course, she was overjoyed to see us, and we spent about an hour with her, but then we went away and left her there for the balance of the quarantine. It must have been a tremendous disappointment for the dog.

On completion of the contract, I was told my next job was not ready, and to go to the office in Crawley. I did this for a few weeks when one day I was called into the manager's office and asked the question, "How would you like to go to Hong Kong?". I knew there was a contract there for a gasworks installation as I had been working on some of the paperwork for the site. My answer was instant, and I said, "I wouldn't!". There was no more conversation, but I heard later in the day, although not officially, that I had refused to go! I did not see it like that. I was asked how would I like to go? but if I had been presented with an air ticket and told to go, I would have had no option but to accept, as I had a mortgage to pay plus other commitments. Having returned home from South Africa I had no desire to go to other parts of the World.

New Toyota Plant

My next job was to join the rest of the team to commission the new Toyota plant at Burnaston near Derby. I was immediately puzzled as despite my experience with steam, I was not allowed in the boiler house! Mainly I was filing documents and drawings, but I was also responsible for Lifts, Doors, and Overhead Cranes, and I was not comfortable with this!

Nearer the end of my time on the contract I received a phone call while at home on a weekend. I was told to go to the site on Sunday as they wished to test the 12-inch steam main for leaks, but it would be confirmed later. I did not get confirmation, so I went to site on the Monday morning as usual and was told that the test had been cancelled.

Later in the week the test was started, but I did not agree with the process being used, and I was not involved anyway! I got the impression that these desk-driving engineers had no idea how to go about it, and the test was eventually abandoned as several leaks appeared even at a very low pressure, and work was required to make the steam main secure. I had been on site for a year when a new project was handed to me.

Faslane Nuclear Submarine Base

Back to Scotland again, and I was somewhat puzzled. My security pass had been withdrawn while I was at Aldermaston, where the warheads for the Trident missiles were manufactured, yet here I was at the submarine base where the ships that used them were docked and maintained, apparently securely employed! After four years my security had obviously improved!

It was hard work for the Toyota again using virtually the same route, plus a little further. Leaving the site at 14:30 on a Friday meant I arrived back in Ipswich around Midnight due to the Rush hour at almost every place enroute, but the car performed magnificently. Similarly, I would leave home at 18:00 on Sunday to be back at my digs in Helensburgh at 00:45 where I would indulge in an alcoholic libation to enable me to relax for a few hours' sleep, and I would be on site at my desk at 06:30. There was less traffic late on a Sunday, so faster progress could be made.

Julie made a couple of visits back to the UK, and one of them included her prospective husband. He obviously had second thoughts and reneged on the proposal after the wedding dress had been purchased! He took a one-way ticket back to South Africa!

At one of those visits, she bought a Vauxhall car so she could get about, but she also had other plans for it. While working as a barmaid at a village pub we received a message that she had broken down on the way home and needed help. The Toyota was up on blocks with all the wheels removed, so we hired a taxi to take us to the spot, but on arrival the car could not be found, so we went back home in the taxi only to find that Julie was not there either! I have lost count of the number of times we passed each other going in opposite directions until the situation was resolved. Sometime later she traded in the Vauxhall for an MGBGT which she intended taking back to South Africa.

The MG needed some attention and since I was Julie's mechanic, I thought it would help if she knew something about maintaining her car while she was in South Africa where I would not be available. I taught her a few basic things, but before she left with the car, I had the job of giving it a complete respray.

About this time the company where David worked relocated to a place near Reading and the family moved to Berkshire. They finally settled in Finchampstead near Wokingham, and our reason for settling in Ipswich disappeared.

LETTING OFF STEAM

A mini power station was under construction at Eye in Suffolk and the boilers were burning coal mixed with chicken litter. The company was looking for staff and I considered my 'Unit Ticket', that qualified me to drive a big ship, would be sufficient to allow me to run the control room of this plant, so I applied for a job. It seems I was right because I received a telephonic reply asking me to go for an interview.

Unfortunately, the only time mutually for this was while I was at work in Scotland, but a telephonic interview was suggested, and I waited to be contacted. Since I heard nothing further, I queried the lack of contact, and was told that the post had been filled, but another plant was being built at Thetford, and I should apply for that! This was disappointing as a daily drive to Eye from Ipswich was a lot more convenient than one to Thetford, instead of a weekly drive to and from Scotland.

British Coal advertised a post for someone to maintain the new static grate they had introduced for coal-fired boilers. I took a days' sick leave for an interview in Tewksbury and was selected for the job although the salary was poor compared with the one being paid by Babcock, but I was sick of the deskwork, and wanted to get 'my hands dirty' again. I submitted my notice to Babcock Contractors and accepted the post at British Coal.

Chapter 15

A range of jobs

British Coal

A company car was provided so the Toyota got a break and allowed Fay the use of a car. My office was in Warrington, which was a long drive every Monday morning, however my immediate boss was not particular about time, and very often we would meet on site at various places around the country.

I was told that I would not be expected to have full knowledge of the project for at least 6 months, but as it happened, I was fully conversant in less than 3 months, pleasing my boss immensely as it lightened his physical load. I was used to chain grates and underfeed stokers when it came to burning coal, but now I was dealing with Top Feed boilers, something I had never seen before.

The new static grate had been handed to various boiler houses around the country, mostly in the North of England, and I spent a lot of my time there. I found it difficult to find accommodation each time that fitted British Coal's budget, and in one case I found it easier to drive home from Birmingham and return the following morning!

I cannot say that I enjoyed the job as once again I saw very little of the home I was buying with the constant travelling, but disappointing news was heading in my direction. After 7 months British Coal decided to end the project and the job I had disappeared!

Unemployed again, and this time I was in no position to pay my monthly mortgage payments, and Fay could not manage that on her own. I made visits to the Job Centre in Ipswich, but there were very little on offer, and the dole money wouldn't keep me in cigarettes, so I gave up smoking! Strangely, I found it quite easy to give up after forty years, despite what I had been told, but really, I haven't given up smoking, I have given up buying cigarettes!

After a couple of months, I found a job for a pump engineer advertised in the Job Centre and made an application for it. I was granted an interview and armed with the documentation supplied by the Royal Navy I drove to Colchester.

This was a new venture, but I did not see it as being too difficult. The company manufactured bespoke chillers and wanted to diversify into the pump world. It was close to home, and I would be sleeping in my own bed every night, which was a change from the previous few years! It was also my first adventure into self-employment in the UK.

Tritherm Engineering

I accepted the job, and having arrived for work, I was sent to a site in Baldock where pumps were to be installed in two wells. Since I was self-employed, I had to use my own transport, so the Toyota was also employed as well. I was accompanied by a colleague in a similar position, skilled in civil work, who lived in Colchester, and each day I would collect him on my way to Baldock as he had no transport.

There was little to do on site, and no materials to work with for several days, but we were required to be there. I think we were there for roughly 6 months all told, but after

2 months we became employed by the company and put on a salary. I was very grateful for the 2 months self-employment as the salary, plus the fees for the use of the car, allowed me to pay the deficit on the mortgage, and also buy two airline tickets for Fay and I to return to South Africa.

The reason for the return to South Africa was that Rory was getting married to Carol, and as Julie had decided to stay when we left, we would spend Christmas with her in Bushman's River. It was an opportunity to meet Carol's parents and brothers whom we had not met, and after the wedding we hired a car and drove from Johannesburg to Bushman's River. Afterwards we drove to Cape Town where Fay had never been and later flew back to the UK.

After completion of the Baldock contract, I was sent to Edmonton Sewage Treatment Works with a large team. I drove to Colchester each morning where I parked my car and boarded a small bus that drove us to site, and after the days' work, it was a return trip to Colchester where I could collect my car. All in all, a fourteen-hour day.

> ... *if the pit flooded, ... I should drop whatever I was doing and get out as quickly as possible as the sewage could rise faster than one could run up the steps!*

There were multiple diesel engines being fuelled by gas that was produced by the treatment process, each engine driving a pump, or generator, or some machine involved in the process. The pumps were 60 feet below the engine and driven by shafting. Some of the engines were being replaced while others were being overhauled by our crew, and pump drives also being maintained.

Back to a welding machine while I was constructing pipework for the new engines being installed, and that made a pleasing change. I was also involved in the maintenance of the shafting to several pumps. One particular job gave me a lot of satisfaction where I had to instal small-bore stainless-steel piping down a pit, from some monitoring instruments at the surface down to equipment at the bottom. I was warned that if the pit flooded, as it did from time to time, I should drop whatever I was doing and get out as quickly as possible as the sewage could rise faster than one could run up the steps!

It all came to an end one day after almost 2 years. We all gathered at the workshop in Colchester and were told that the company had to close although no reasons were given. With selected individuals, management intended opening the following day as a different company! As the contract had not run the entire 2 years, we were not paid any redundancy money and were unemployed.

Tritherm Engineering continued normally, as we were just a subsidiary group within it. However, the parent company, where we had been contracted, wanted our work at Edmonton to be completed, and were prepared to use our labour if we could find an agreement of terms. I was elected as spokesman, and a work force was set up, and used to complete the outstanding work, that would reduce in pairs as each job was finished.

I was unemployed again but this time it did not affect me so badly, and I was able to continue paying my way. I kept in touch with the selected group in Colchester, as they were the only local people who had any knowledge of my capabilities, and eventually I was offered employment with them. They had contacts with the water utility companies and needed a pump engineer.

Tritech Engineering

I started off constructing and welding a cover for a well at a site in Dover. The cover was four metres diameter and contained two supports of twelve by 6-inch RSJs, and working alone, this took me some time as the entire structure had to be covered in steel chequer plating. I was later replaced as a welder and became the specialist pump engineer. Usually, I would have to strip a pump, take it to a firm that would sand blast the interior, and then paint the internal body with an epoxy coating that would improve the efficiency of the pump after I had reassembled it.

Our new welder was a MIG welder whereas I was just using electrodes. I'm not a fan of MIG welding as it seems to me that it doesn't deliver the penetration but is a lot quicker. On two occasions I had to deliver piping for powder coating to a firm in Dudley and I could see that the weld had not penetrated through to the inside of the seam! I was surprised that they were accepted for the powder coating process.

Then, an ad appeared for heating engineers at an RAF station. I found it coincidental that the persons interviewing me were originally from Associated Heating Services (AHS) where I had applied all those years before, yet I did not recognise any of them.

Heatsave

I was back to shiftwork again! Now I was on a shift of two individuals as the mechanical engineer with Mike Bruce, who was the electrical engineer, at RAF Lakenheath which is an American base working with the RAF. It was a 12-hour shift for 4 days at a time, and one of us on call for the remaining 12 hours each day. My opposite number on the other shift was earmarked for a management course and I had to stand in for him for the next 3 weeks, which turned out to be a continuous shift of 4 weeks! The salary was not spectacular either, but it did mean that I slept in my own bed every night, as long as I was not on call! As Mike and I lived near each other, we took turns in sharing the transport to and from the base while we were on shift.

I guess there isn't a lot of use for steam on an air base, but I found the Americans I had to work with were particularly ignorant of it. The only use for steam was medical, the hospital with the connected boiler house, and dentistry with autoclaves. I tested the boiler water every morning and ensured two of the boilers were operating efficiently, with a third on standby or down for maintenance. Both Mike and I would walk around the hospital to make sure everything was working OK, otherwise it was a case of planned maintenance for equipment spread around the base and callouts. It was what I call clipboard engineering, and I rarely had to get my hands dirty.

The base was like a part of the United States, so there were schools, shops and houses although they were maintained on a different contract. The only concession to British life was that vehicles drove on the left-hand side of the road.

The Toyota Cressida was fifteen years old by this time and would have cost far too much to get it through an MOT inspection, so we went shopping for a replacement. I was of the opinion that there was only two of us, so why did we need a vehicle with more than two seats? I was keen to find a Toyota MR2 as I had seen them while I was working on the Toyota project with Babcock Contractors. We eventually found the one we were looking for at a garage in Norwich and we shared the cost by buying with cash and a Credit card! It was comfortable and warm to drive home since the Cressida's heater had given up working some months previously.

It was disappointing and boring work, and I noticed an advertisement for a Commissioning engineer at a local company, so I applied for the job. I was accepted, but when the paperwork arrived, I was not satisfied with the job description, and I told them I was not interested. A few days later a different job description was offered, and I was happy with that, so accepted the job.

Kings Boiler Hire

There is a difference between the job description of a commissioning engineer in the UK and South Africa that puzzled me. In the UK the job would be better suited to someone with an electrical background, and I found that a lot of my work was of an electrical nature with this new company. Where they could get an electrician with combustion experience was beyond me, but I found the job to be quite demanding with the limitations of my electrical knowledge.

I was also at odds with the management when I was sent to a job some considerable distance away, only to find the fault was gas related, and I was not gas qualified as far as the British regulations were concerned. It did not prevent me from doing a sound job, but I was not happy about having to do it, and I wrote a letter to them saying that if I ended up being prosecuted for it, then the management would be standing next to me in court. This of course did not go down well, and we were at loggerheads for several months until I forced the issue in getting them to fire me rather than resign!

Heatsave again

Heatsave were advertising for staff on a different contract to the one where I had been employed previously at RAF Lakenheath, and an interview was not required after my previous two years with them. Now I was servicing schools, shops and accommodation, but no steam work at all. There were still lots of boilers of varying sizes, but only for heating central heating systems, plus lots of calorifiers. With the schools being part of this there was kitchen equipment to service, and I was even "borrowed" by the MOD staff to diagnose and fix problems with heating problems in one of the aircraft hangers. There was also a restaurant and a theatre for us to maintain. I also view hamburgers in a different light now having had to work behind the scenes on the other side of the counter!

It was about this time that Fay became quite concerned that we would still be paying a mortgage even when we were in our eighties! Would we be able to pay, and still be capable of being employed? We paid a visit to Citizens Advice Bureaux, and were advised to terminate the mortgage, and what then? A visit to Ipswich Council to see if help would be available, and given similar advice, so we put the house on the market after I had replaced the kitchen with a complete renewal.

The house was eventually sold, and we sought help from Ipswich Council, only to be told by the same people who advised us to sell, that no help was available since we had made ourselves homeless!!! We left Ipswich after Fay worked her magic again and found us somewhere to live in Great Finborough, in what her grandchildren called the Enid Blyton house. I was closer to work now living in a village just outside Stowmarket.

Fay had also conspired with my employers for me to have two weeks holiday and had packed a suitcase…

Colin dropped in at Trafalgar Close to visit Fay as a former secretary, and as Fate would have it, met Julie. This was to lead to a fascinating period of events that finally led to their marriage in 2000.

As a sixty-fifth birthday surprise for me, Fay had organised a trip on a narrow boat with Colin and Julie, as well as secretly inviting Rory and Carol to come with us. It was not possible for Carol to come, so her place was taken by my sister-in-law, June. Fay had also conspired with my employers for me to have two weeks holiday and had packed a suitcase of my clothes for what I thought was a visit to Colin and Julie for a weekend. We did a tour of the 'Warwickshire Loop', which was very pleasant and a great surprise, especially to see my son again. He had to leave us at Leamington Spa to attend to some business in

London but joined us later in Stowmarket after we had gone back home.

As a result of being rent payers, Fay would go into the Council offices regularly to ensure our names were on the list for people who needed help for housing. We lived in Great Finborough for a year and moved into Stowmarket to a more convenient bungalow. While there we were invited to a wedding in the United States. Now we were living in the UK, Fay's sister Wendy had crossed the Atlantic several times, as she had done previously, to visit from Toronto, and Fay thought the wedding invitation gave us an opportunity to respond by visiting Wendy at the same time. The bride was a friend of Julie and a word to her obtained an invitation to the wedding for Wendy, who became our chauffeuse in Canada and the USA.

Wendy entertained us all quite magnificently driving the four of us to places of interest around Toronto, and then from there into Ohio for the wedding where Fay and I would stand in as the bride's parents, who would not be attending, in 2002. Crossing the border at Detroit proved a little stressful with belligerent security staff which cured me of any desire for further return trips to the USA! On the return we had a more convivial passage via Buffalo, and we viewed Niagara Falls which is grossly commercialised.

Fay and I also made several trips to South Africa, in particular to Rory and Carol's wedding in 1994, and Rory's fortieth birthday celebration 2004, where we continued on a tour of South Africa with a work colleague, 'Rusty' Russell, and Hazel his wife, from Johannesburg to Cape Town. This included visits to a number of game reserves and other places of interest on the way, with an excellent tour guide.

Chapter 16

Tragedy

Fay

We had been granted a two-bedroom bungalow in Gislingham and were about to move there. I took Fay her early morning cup of tea before I headed off to work one morning and told her that she had been wheezing while asleep, and after I had gone, she made an appointment with the doctor. When I got home that evening, I was told what she had done, and that the diagnosis was not good, and Fay had been referred to Ipswich hospital for tests!

Cancer

We attended Ipswich hospital the next day, and Fay underwent several tests and examinations. At the end of it Fay was told she had lung cancer, and that was the start of several visits until she met a surgeon who informed her that the only remedy was to remove her left lung.

This would be done in the Norfolk and Norwich hospital, and we drove there the next day. Julie came down from her home in Leicestershire and the two of us spent a stressful period waiting to hear the result of the operation. I had stopped going to work without asking for permission, and since I was approaching seventy, I guessed it would not be long before I was going to be replaced anyway. I visited Fay every day and she was in good spirits after the operation.

Jacky and David were coming to stay for the weekend and visit Fay in hospital. On the way back from the Norwich hospital, one of the cables for the gear shift in the MR2 broke with the car in second gear, and I could not select any other, so I had to call for assistance from the AA again.

Luckily, I was only a few miles from home and the AA man managed to get the car into third gear, making it quicker to drive but very difficult to get the car going and I could smell the clutch burning! The AA man followed me all the way home to make sure I made it and got home in time to meet Jacky and David when they arrived. The next day I stripped the car down, ordered a new cable and fitted it myself. Luckily, I still had the company van and used it to visit Fay in hospital while waiting for the car's spare parts to arrive.

"How long have I got?", and I'll never forget the reply...

January 2006. We had to make regular visits to Ipswich hospital where Fay had to undergo treatment of chemotherapy, until she was told that the treatment was not working, and it was going to be stopped. We were told there was no alternative, and Fay asked the question, **"How long have I got?"**, and I'll never forget the reply, **"Who knows? Maybe 6, or 60 months"**. It was devastating news and was not a happy drive back home.

Fay took to her bed and continued to receive treatment from our local GP who made house calls. The main treatment was Morphine as the painkiller and initially 20 mg, but as the pain increased, she was offered a bigger dose, the doctor told her she could go to 200 mg, if necessary, but she refused! Her reason was, "I don't want to become an addict."! How do you tell a person who is dying that there is no danger of becoming an addict?

There was an embarrassing moment for Fay, and it was necessary to call for an ambulance, and she was taken off to Ipswich hospital again. We were getting to know the place quite well now and I was allowed to sit with her while they searched for a suitable ward for her, and when one was allocated, I went home, knowing the name of the ward and where it was.

Later in the day I returned for the normal visiting hours only to find Fay had been moved to a different ward, and a different part of the hospital. It was July, and the UK was experiencing a heat wave so it must have been very uncomfortable lying in bed. I had a difference of opinion with the hospital staff, in that I was not allowed to go out to buy an electric fan to keep Fay cool, as nobody was available to sanction the use of an unauthorised electrical item to be connected to the hospital power supply, even though it was a brand-new item!!!

Then on a visit I found Fay in tears when I arrived. Someone had told her she was in an "End of Life" ward, and later I was called into an office where I was asked if she should be resuscitated if she passed away! I spent the rest of the visit trying to comfort Fay, but I doubt my efforts were a lot of use.

As soon as I got home, I advised Jacky and Julie of the situation, and both of them came to be with her as soon as they could. We were allowed continuous visiting over the last few days, and even provided with a room with a bed where we could stay overnight if required. I told Jacky and Julie to make use of it, and I sat in the chair next to

Fay's bed most of the time, but by this time she was heavily sedated, and no conversation possible.

Losing Fay

And so, I lost my one True Love on 25th July 2006. The three of us were at her bedside when the final moment arrived. Jacky came to stay with me for a few days and helped me go through the process of organising the funeral and the legal requirements. We were given a date of 8th August 2006 for Fay's cremation at Ipswich crematorium, and it was well attended by relatives and friends she had made over the years. Wendy made a return visit too, who had been here earlier in the year.

Julie and Colin asked me what I intended to do now I was alone? I had no relatives in East Anglia, and they were curious to know if I was going to remain in Suffolk or move to a spot closer to relatives that lived in Herefordshire, or the surrounding area. I assured them that I had no thoughts of moving anywhere else as Fay and I had established this as our home. Colin was nearing the end of his project of converting the property in Leicestershire, and they had been considering moving to Suffolk anyway. This they eventually did and bought a property outside Mendham.

One night in September I experienced a severe pain in my back that prevented me from sleeping. I spent a lot of time considering whether I should call for an ambulance, but eventually I was able to get through the night, and an appointment at my local health centre where I got pain relief and was referred to West Suffolk hospital for an X-ray. It was assumed I had a kidney stone, and was given an MRI scan, but this revealed nothing at the time.

Later, another one of these overran the area being scanned and revealed a problem with the lining at the base of my lungs. I was diagnosed with Pleural Plaques, which meant I had to make regular quarterly appointments for observation of the complaint that lasted for 3 years.

This eventually culminated in Julie taking me for a visit to Papworth hospital for some precisely accurate measurements, and a biopsy of the fluid around the lung to be taken. I was later advised that there was no sign of cancer, and there would be no further development of the pleural plaques and the future visits to the hospital were cancelled.

Tours of South Africa

In 2010 I ventured back to South Africa on my own, with an invitation to spend Easter with Rory, Carol, and Russell and his family. Rory and Carol returned to their home in Johannesburg after a few days, and I paid a visit to East London. Steve offered me the use of his annex and I was able to spend some time with Terry and his family too. They all did an excellent job of entertaining me before I drove back to Port Elizabeth.

In all the years I lived in South Africa I did not ever visit the Victoria Falls, and I had to meet up with Rory again in a few days, so I used the interval to visit the Falls. Although there is a little commercialisation, it is nothing like it is at Niagara, and the area around the Falls is quite natural. I seem to have chosen the wrong time of year to visit, as there was a lot of water which causes a tremendous spray, and the Falls are almost invisible because of it. It is better to view later in the year, maybe in September.

I returned to Johannesburg and was then taken on a one-day trip to Sun City, which is like an oasis in the African bush. A drive to the north of the country where we spent some days in a property at Hans Merensky, belonging to Carol's brother Peter.

This was something special, as it is situated on the edge of a lake where wildlife, including Hippopotamus and Crocodiles, are free to enter the garden area. A tour of the golf course showed that this hazard also existed there, which gave a round of golf an added interest! We spent a day cruising through The Kruger National Park, and had breakfast cooked on a barbeque at one of the rest camps. I returned to the UK having been thoroughly entertained.

In 2013 Julie mildly nagged me to take her back to South Africa to reminisce and meet old friends, and we made an independent tour from Johannesburg to Cape Town via East London and Port Elizabeth, having been entertained by Rory and Carol. My main object was to get access to funds I had left there, which helped to finance our trip, and Rory's help was invaluable. We also paid a visit to Val's nephew, Russell, and his family when we passed through Port Elizabeth.

At the end of 2014 I got a message telling me that Steve was very ill with cancer and was not expected to survive for more than a few weeks. I was hesitant in making another trip to South Africa so soon after the previous visit although I really would have wanted to be with my old friend. My reluctance to go right away cost me the chance to be at his bedside as I did eventually decide to go, and Steve died while I was travelling to see him in January 2015. I attended the funeral at the crematorium with his family.

I was invited to use the annex at Steve's home for my accommodation and gratefully accepted the offer. I met old friends at the dog club, which had changed quite considerably, and had split from the GSD club, and KUSA, due to changes in the system of training and judging. I also visited Terry and his wife Memory, and was entertained and invited to stay with them for some time. Rory was able to spend a weekend with me, and I drove to Port Elizabeth to make it easier for him. This also gave us the opportunity to spend some time with Russell and his family, before I drove back to East London, and home to the UK.

This became a very sad period in my life as the following year I was told that Terry was dying, but because I had spent so much time with him during my visit for Steve, I did not make another trip to South Africa to be with him. Also in the UK, my aunt Gwen and uncle Bert both, in their nineties, and the last of the previous generation of Barkers, passed away during this time. This leaves me and Thelma as the seniors of our present generation.

Chapter 17

How much longer?

COPD

I was now classed as having Chronic Obstructive Pulmonary Disease, and a while later I was offered the chance to join a twelve-week rehabilitation course. It took place two days per week in Bury St Edmunds, and after a couple of classes I felt that I was there under false pretences, as all my course mates had to have some form of medical assistance to breathe! I enjoyed the course, which was really just mild exercise, and started me on a daily routine of walking some distance. Initially this was at least two miles per day but developed into a minimum of one hundred kilometres per month. Quite frequently the daily walk was closer to four miles each day, but then one day I found that I had to stop for a rest after just one mile! I felt that this was significant and made an appointment at the local health centre.

Pacemaker

On 29th November 2018 I was told I needed a pacemaker and would need to go to West Suffolk hospital immediately for the operation! The staff were persuaded to allow me to take my car home as long as I kept my appointment at the hospital, and once again Julie came to the rescue, dropped what she was doing, and drove me to the hospital in Bury St Edmunds. I was kept in overnight and was first in the operating theatre the next day when a pacemaker was placed in my chest. As usual, when it came to being discharged from the hospital, my blood pressure was exceptionally high, and I was kept in for a further night. I understand I have a complaint called "White Coat Syndrome", and whenever I get near a medical building my blood pressure rises excessively, and I was discharged the next day after being supplied with medication to reduce my blood pressure and advised to visit my doctor. I am still taking the medication on the advice of the doctor!

The Covid virus arrived in the UK, and so far, it has passed me by, but the rules for associating with other people curtailed my travels around the country. I used to make at least annual visits to see my uncle Bert and May in Bristol, and also to Ross on Wye to visit Thelma and Jean. Over the years I have met other members of the family still living in the area, but generally it has been for a funeral.

... now waiting for the right eye to be done in the New Year with great anticipation, when perhaps I will only need glasses for reading, if at all.

Before I left South Africa, I found there was a problem with my sight, as I was finding it difficult to read the information plate inside the boiler panels, and a visit to an optician for an eye test meant I needed spectacles for reading. On arrival in the UK an optician advised me that I needed to wear glasses to drive a vehicle, and over the years the glasses needed updating as my eyesight deteriorated. This was due to cataracts in both of my eyes, and as I grew older, so they grew stronger, until the optician asked me if I was prepared to have an operation to have them removed. I liked the idea of improved vision and agreed to have the left eye done in July 2021, strongly contributing to better vision. I am now waiting for the right eye to be done in the New Year with great anticipation, when perhaps I will only need glasses for reading, if at all.

Rory was hoping he could find a suitable job in the UK made plans to settle here, even on a temporary basis. Carol has a problem in that she can only travel on a South African passport, which means she has to undergo tests to satisfy the immigration authorities if she wishes to reside in this country. Rory, owning a British passport has none of these problems, and found a company that was prepared to employ him, so he planned to visit and work here for a 12-month period to check it all out. Unfortunately, the company gave him menial work to do, even though he was employed in a senior position, and he became bored and frustrated with it. It was great to have my son in the country, but as it didn't work out, he returned to South Africa after the twelve-month period was over.

I was having regular check-ups for my COPD condition, and I was asked if I would like to participate in another course. I accepted the offer quite eagerly, and this time it was held in Eye, so I didn't have to drive so far.

I was fortunate to have Rory's company when I experienced severe pain in my abdomen, and he drove me to Ipswich hospital where I was diagnosed with appendicitis. Had he not been here, no doubt Julie and Colin would have come to the rescue as they usually do, but it saved them the inconvenience. My course was cancelled after only a couple of sessions, but I was handed a new one after a recuperation period from hospital, and I enjoyed it as much as the first course.

I am approaching the end of my story, but this is not the end of my life yet. I consider that despite all the setbacks, small as they are. I have been a very lucky person. I have been granted good health with only minor ailments, and although I live alone now there are people who care about my wellbeing, and I wish it to continue as long as I am able to do the things I enjoy for as long as possible. There are regrets of course, and the one that really annoys me even today, was leaving the Royal Navy so early. The 25 years in South Africa as the alternative were not entirely satisfactory, but it was an interesting and instructive experience. Ipswich was never my choice of where we should finally live on returning from South Africa, but circumstances made that decision, and quite honestly, I have no thoughts about where else it should have been.

My one big regret is that Fay and I were not allowed to be together for a longer period. In our younger days, cousins were not meant to be lovers, and any thoughts of marriage were unthinkable, so we went our separate ways, but Fate was not to be denied. Even so, it interfered and cut our time short, unfairly for Fay, since I was as guilty as she, if not more so when it came to smoking, which was the cause of her cancer. I was 70 years old when she died, and she was 67.

Personal likes and dislikes

> ... *what has happened to my patience... but now the least little thing chases it away and I become an irritable old man. Shirt buttons are a case in point...*

I don't know what has happened to my patience which used to be unlimited! Maybe it was all used up during the years living with Valerie, but now the least little thing chases it away and I become an irritable old man. Shirt buttons are a case in point, and sometimes I think I am in my second childhood because doing them up or undoing them become major problems, whereas a little patience is all that is needed.

Computers could have something to do with my lack of patience. I have never come across anything that is more frustrating than a computer when it will not do what it is being asked to do. I understand that it is only as good as the information that is being fed into it but sometimes it appears to defy logic!

I don't paint or sketch anymore either and both of these pastimes need and can instil patience but as I am not creative, I cannot think of anything to put on canvas. I remember a time a couple of years ago when I set everything up to paint a picture and could not think of anything to paint before I put any paint on my palette, so I put everything away again!

I used to enjoy listening to Fay play the piano whether it was classical or the up-to-date popular music, but it was perhaps the one thing where we differed. I was raised during the era of the big band, and I love the music, and I find the popular style today of a few twanging guitars rather insipid compared with the rich harmony of the instruments in a big band. Fay was a lover of Rock and Roll and pop music whereas I have no interest in it at all. I am a great believer in discipline too, and feel that the modern entertainer lacks respect, and insults the audience with their presentation compared with the smartness of a uniformed big band.

I am happy listening to the popular classics as well as jazz, whether it is traditional or a smooth piano and saxophone, but not really modern jazz. I prefer black coffee and cannot remember how many years since I last had a cup of tea. I am a lover of chocolate, but I am disciplined enough to keep it in check. I like an alcoholic drink and usually have a "sundowner" each evening but certainly do not overdo it, maybe I should say anymore.

I am a rotten holidaymaker and as I love to drive my car, I find it more fun going and coming back, although I am not keen on flying to my destination! As far as holidaymaking goes, I am not a fan of the beach or sunbathing, but prefer to visit interesting places but I don't find it fun on my own, yet generally I do not get tired of my own company.

Now, at the age of 87, and a great believer in the Family, I try to keep in touch with both the Deacon and Barker families. The Deacons seem to be spread worldwide and I must succumb to email or such, but the Barkers are still mainly in the area of Herefordshire.

In the meantime, I can only say, "To be continued".

LETTING OFF STEAM

Printed in Great Britain
by Amazon